Working Girl

Working Girl

On Selling Art and Selling Sex

Sophia Giovannitti

London • New York

This paperback edition first published by Verso 2025
First published by Verso 2023

The manufacturer's authorized representative in the EU
for product safety (GPSR) is LOGOS EUROPE,
9 rue Nicolas Poussin, 17000, La Rochelle, France
contact@logoseurope.eu

1 3 5 7 9 10 8 6 4 2

Verso
UK: 6 Meard Street, London W1F 0EG
US: 207 East 32nd Street, New York, NY 10016
versobooks.com

Verso is the imprint of New Left Books

ISBN-13: 978-1-83976-671-8
ISBN-13: 978-1-83976-672-5 (UK EBK)
ISBN-13: 978-1-83976-673-2 (US EBK)

British Library Cataloguing in Publication Data
A catalogue record for this book is available from the British Library

The Library of Congress Has Cataloged the Hardback Edition as Follows:

Names: Giovannitti, Sophia, author.
Title: Working girl : on selling art and selling sex / Sophia Giovannitti.
Description: London ; New York : Verso, 2023. | Includes bibliographical references.
Identifiers: LCCN 2022056902 (print) | LCCN 2022056903 (ebook) | ISBN 9781839766701 (hardback) | ISBN 9781839766732 (US ebook) | ISBN 9781839766725 (UK ebook)
Subjects: LCSH: Sex work—Social aspects. | Prostitution—Social aspects. | Selling—Art. | Art—Economic aspects. | Art and society.
Classification: LCC HQ118 .G556 2023 (print)
| LCC HQ118 (ebook) | DDC
306.74—dc23/eng/20230126
LC record available at https://lccn.loc.gov/2022056902
LC ebook record available at https://lccn.loc.gov/2022056903

Typeset in Sabon by Biblichor Ltd, Scotland
Printed and bound by CPI Group (UK) Ltd, Croydon CR0 4YY

For David Justice, who taught me about anarchism and true love,
and for anyone who's ever turned a trick.

Try imagining a world worth living in.

—Leslie Feinberg, *Stone Butch Blues*

He's comming [sic] to meet me on Sun. Can't wait!! . . . Please God let him love me!! . . . This could be it [five happy faces] . . . Hes [sic] going to publish my pictures I'm so glad I didn't sleep with him either! . . . I hate for men to want sex all the time. I hate sex anyway.

—Anna Nicole Smith, diary entry in advance of a meeting with Paul Marciano, head of Guess

On the left, the economy had traditionally been seen as the opposite of art, just as the act of selling is the opposite of the spontaneous gift. But the aesthetic strategies of the "counter-culture"—difference and otherness, the rhizome, the proliferation of subjectivities—could be exalted and set to work. The margins become the center; the art of transgression becomes the commodity.

—Brian Holmes, *Unleashing the Collective Phantoms: Essays in Reverse Imagineering*

Contents

On Meaning, Part I

The first sex worker I ever (knowingly) met wouldn't, I don't think, have called herself that. In colloquial terms, she was an art girl, and if she was a worker at all, she was the kind who liked to fall in love with her clients. Ever pretentious, she would joke that the guy responsible for paying her rent was trying to turn her "into a capitalist," which, frankly, didn't seem like much of a transformation. She called relationships "durational performance art pieces." We met through acquaintances, and, intrigued by projects she was working on, I pursued a friendship; it was short-lived.

By the time I met this girl, I'd been edging my way toward sex work for a while. It's hard for me to remember the details of how and why, now, not because it was so long ago, but because once you have done something that comes to define a large part of your identity, it's difficult to recall exactly what you thought about that thing before doing it. I know that on a practical level, I understood it as the best way to make a lot of money in a short amount of time, and I knew I needed to find a solution to my near-categorical hatred of work. I allowed myself to think of it initially as an art project, probably to rationalize a choice I was told was risky and to protect myself from the stigma that would come from making that choice. Making art can justify a recklessness that making money doesn't. And it combined two things I spent an inordinate amount of time thinking about—sex and capitalism.

Naively, I thought I might dip my toe into the blurred lines of the market by selling a dual performance with my new friend. Something wherein we wouldn't actually have to fuck clients, but could sell an allure, a way that they could watch us. To her credit, she didn't see how this would benefit her financially any more than the situation she had already created: dating men who were likable enough, who had more money than they knew what to do with and less access to women than they knew how to deal with, and who would gladly pay for a lifestyle that could support her making art. She was right—it wouldn't have—and we never worked together. As consolation, I suppose, for rejecting my offer, she gave me a book called *The Art of Seduction*. I only ever used it to prop open my broken window. It was stacked on top of a classic client-to-his-creative-hooker gift: Patti Smith's *Just Kids*. The books rotted on my windowsill for years.

Nonetheless intrigued, I followed her example and joined SeekingArrangement—the inevitable first step of the naive, collegiate, full-service sex worker—filling in the career box with "artist." Still unsure about selling sex, I decided I was just in it for the experience. I met a married man for afternoon drinks who called himself an author and explicitly stated in his profile that he wasn't looking for a pro. I wore a new white dress I still have, though it fits me differently now. After two Aperol spritzes, we walked a block together and he took my hand and asked if he could kiss me. I looked at my hand in his, and I felt neither attraction to him nor curiosity about him, the two things that would normally lead me to kiss someone.

Even at the time, knowing so little and still feeling reluctant to become the kind of professional he reviled, I felt viscerally that to kiss him for free would be an experience that would give me nothing in return, save for regret. I was slightly nervous to say no—he was standing close enough to me that it seemed he'd already taken my yes for granted—but I still said it, and pulled away, and left soon after. In the days following, though I'd refused the kiss, thoughts of irritation and regret shadowed me, specifically around the fact that I hadn't been paid: *Why did I gave this guy my time, for free?* I wondered. I knew vaguely that I wasn't simply looking to have affairs with married men, but I couldn't yet admit to myself the straightforwardness of what, exactly, I wanted.

In the beginning of my working life, I felt that I wanted to find a patron, not a client, and I wanted to sell a performance, not sex. I'm not sure what the physical difference was to me—I think I imagined there would be no penetration—but the actual relevant demarcation I know I made was between how the two scenarios might feel, and what those feelings would mean. If I wasn't straightforwardly selling sex, I reasoned, but something more nuanced and shrouded, my relationship to sex, to myself as a woman, and to the world would not have to change quite so much.

The two scenarios, in the end, did feel different from one another, just not in the way I'd anticipated—the performance-patron route simply felt like a lot more work, for a lot less money, wherein I was tasked with either deflecting requests for full-service or persuading someone that tipping me for my company wasn't transactional but merely supportive. My friend, the capitalist, told me that unappealing men become *hotter* when they're handing you cash. Sadly, cash has yet to turn me on. It's just something I need.

My first real sex work experience ended up being both blessedly well-circumstanced and entirely unglamorous: I acted as a third for a queer graduate student and her buttoned-up, graying sugar daddy, licking his ass in a studio apartment he kept in Midtown for just such an occasion. I walked away after ninety minutes with a grand in an unmarked envelope, more than I'd ever made in a week, let alone a day or an hour. It wasn't sex, per se, but it wasn't art, either.

The first time I sold sex alone was different. I met a man who proposed a complex allowance system, with amounts depreciating throughout the month and returning to full value at the start of the next month. I agreed, excited to be offered what felt like a contract, signifying my sexual labor as something that existed, though the terms, I realized after, were abysmal. He bought me a book and took me to an oyster bar. I'd never had an oyster before but I swallowed one so as not to look childish. It was salty in a way that made me choke.

He took me up to a hotel room he'd already checked into. It was through him that I learned about Dayuse, a website that partners with various hotels to offer discounted rates for truncated, daytime stays; their "How does it work?" copy reads, "Your hotel room for few hours during the day! Work in peace, get some rest during a layover or experience a few hours away from your usual day-to-day! 1 Dayuse, 1000 possibilities," as though its purpose isn't obvious, and singular.

The room was downtown, adequate but sparse. He had requested that I forgo perfume, something I never wore anyway, and that I leave no visible marks on his body. We had sex, and he smoothed my hair and was gentle, and that was the part I liked the least; it was the first time I realized how much more a stranger's affection bothers me than their lust. Affection is more particular and precious than sex. Afterward he offered me a warm, wet towel—to sponge myself off, I suppose—and he showered. When I got home I cried. It felt like release more than anything; a demarcation of myself moving from *girl* to *prostitute*. I cry at any kind of shift—age, season, move—whether good or bad.

I have many more of these memories, but a lot are opaque to me, having faded into the background and existing only in the recesses of thought. Sometimes they peek through the veil if I walk on a particular block, or smell a particular scent, and then I will marvel at my younger self, throwing herself before all of these people, in all of these places, and trying desperately to understand what it all meant.

There are all kinds of people who trade sex for money, and all kinds of reasons people do so—hugely varied levels of privilege involved, of choice, of coercion. The professional milieu I've found myself in is that of writers and artists living and working in socioeconomically stratified cities where both sex and creative industries thrive, and people who have other options choose to sell sex in order to support a certain kind of life with more free time.

Art and sex occupy similar positions under capitalism. The commodification of each, while rampant, is also rife with anxiety and subject to questions of ethics, purity, and meaning. This is because we are told art and sex shouldn't be commodified. Both are seemingly sacred forms of human expression, and we are taught to keep them close to ourselves, safe from capital's voracious appetite. And yet, art and sex—and specifically the art and sex industries—are actually capital's stress points: two industries saturated in hyper-capitalist relations while also existing on the outskirts of the formal economy. This may explain their profound material similarity: both are filled with wildly stratified price points, scams, blurred legal lines, and exploitation. Art and sex are also connected affectively, through metaphor. Selling art has ever been likened to prostitution—to sell your art is to *prostitute* it—and both traffic in the ability to provoke a particular feeling in another person.

Just as prostitution is the oldest profession, this is the oldest metaphor. I'm trying to figure out what it means to be the metaphor: the prostitute moving through the world of cultural production; the whore at her own exhibit opening; the artist at the gallery dinner one night and the escort at the gallery dinner the next.

When I had yet to sell sex but was planning to start, I confessed to my boyfriend that I worried doing so would irrevocably damage my relationship to sex in my personal life—not because something bad would happen to me, but because I imagined I would disconnect during work-sex, and I didn't want dissociation to become part of my sex life. In other words, I feared I wouldn't have the capacity to differentiate between different kinds of sex in different contexts, and I feared this because it was what I had been told, by movies and articles and concerned friends, over and over. My boyfriend was matter-of-fact about my concern, saying he didn't think I would stop being able to tell the difference between sex with him, for example, and sex with a client. "But how do you know?" I worried. "Because they're different," he answered.

He was right; they are different, and I still know they're different. Selling sex hasn't impacted what sex itself is to me, any more than any other sexual experience I've had; which is to say, of course it has impacted it, but in no unique way. My own sex work has had an equal effect on my sex life as the first person who begged me for head, in high school, citing Kierkegaard's leap of faith as a reason to give it up. I've thought about each with equal fervor and curiosity, wondering, and never knowing, exactly how these experiences have shaped my relationship to desire and coercion. The same goes for making and selling art and writing: I can discern for myself what is meaningful and what is bullshit; what I make that I care dearly for and what I make that is for money alone. I'll never exactly know that my desires operate independent of capitalism—or rather, I'll know that they don't, but this would be true whether or not I ever sold an essay or an artwork in my life. In "Revolutionary Letter #48," Diane di Prima writes,

> sense & sex are boundless & the call
> is to be boundless in them, make the joy
> now, that we want.

The call is to be boundless; I would argue that the path to boundlessness begins with acquiescing to how fully bound we are.

I grew up in a family of artists who refused to commodify their art. Their official position was a principled one: to sell art would be to sell one's soul, tainting an object of unadulterated creation, irreparably, with cash. Offered opportunities at a young age to make money in the art world, my father instead turned to the honest work of construction, believing this would allow him to exist less subsumed by the monster of capitalism. His work was largely devoid of meaning for him, save for the satisfaction of technical expertise; he built homes for wealthy people. As it turned out, his life was subsumed by capitalism, his leisure time swallowed by sixty- and seventy-hour work weeks. His art remained private, produced late at night in our basement, which he turned into his studio. But his art also remained touched by capital in every way, regardless of its refusal to willingly enter the market: flattened into the only pockets of time he could steal from his relentless schedule; restricted by which materials he could afford; abandoned, at a few low points, in his exhaustion, but always returned to; tended to with verve up and against every obstacle. He has made art quietly and dedicatedly for fifty years. His practice, simultaneously pious, constant, and constrained, has been both beautiful and brutal to watch.

From this I learned: there is no escaping capitalism, no protecting our expressions of love and passion from such a totalizing machine. To attempt to protect art and sex from commodification is not only futile; it is also what capitalism insidiously steers us toward for its own benefit. It is in capitalism's best interest for its subjects to maintain a stark separation between work and certain choice expressions of pleasure, because work, then, will always take up more of our time, energy, and resources. The secret that to make pleasure work means it is possible to work less—indeed, the reason so many sell sex, as it provides a higher hourly wage than most other entry-level work—is either kept from our discovery, or painted as unethical. When I say make pleasure work, I mean to sell sex and art—not because doing what you love makes work more bearable, but because the particular economic conditions in these industries facilitate maneuvers and scams that allow people to work less and do what they love more.

I met with a mentor and friend of mine when I was planning a performance piece on work, desirability, and revenge. I had talked to her about hair braiding, and I had sent her a video I made of myself giving my boyfriend head outdoors in upstate New York while the sun was setting, where I look—and there's no other way to describe it—like an angel who is on fire. I wanted her consult. We met at a bar. She showed me how she'd drawn a lovely and crude pen drawing of the video in her notebook, along with sketches of hairbrushes.

This woman is one of the most unusual and smartest people I have ever met. She once began a dance at one venue and had her dancers leave for another venue in the middle. I want to be her; I want to fuck her; I want her to be my mother, and I also want her to physically destroy me—that kind of thing. I don't always take her advice, but I do always cherish it. This time, I took it.

She suggested that I treat my work as a series of studies—ongoing pieces, gestures, and attempts toward a greater whole, without forcing finality or ultimate certainty in any part. In art, a study is traditionally understood to be in service of a finished work but not a finished work itself—rather, a form of preparation; an attempt to understand further. Often shown in retrospectives alongside the final work they preceded, studies might expose the artist's attention to detail, and points of focus, within the process of revelation and excavation. She herself, a choreographer and dancer, had executed many studies. She said it to me somewhat tentatively, as though she was worried she might offend me, but I was hugely relieved. A study spoke to the ongoing nature of what I was working on, and allowed the very ongoingness to be the most interesting part—at least, to me. Every time I thought I found *the thing*—the way to make meaning out of trading sex for money to produce art; the mode through which someone would be forced to acknowledge their power over another, both material and ephemeral; the all-encompassing next topic, whether contracts, or debts, or heterosexuality, or collecting, or self-destruction—I was wrong. Being wrong was ultimately more interesting than being right.

What follows is a series of ruminations based on things I have sold, experienced, made, watched, felt, hated, and wanted. I wish to truly understand the relationship between sex, art, and marketplace, but I have yet to; I imagine it would take a lifetime of study, if even that. What I thought was a fantasy was often indistinguishable from reality; what I thought would hurt me did not, and the opposite was true, too; and what I wanted to be legible was inscrutable. Why this is, I can't yet explain.

In the old biblical fable, two women appear before King Solomon laying claim to the same child. Solomon suggests they cut the baby in two, so each woman can have half, revealing the rightful mother: the one who immediately relinquishes her claim to the baby, giving him up to the other woman so he might remain healthy, whole. To participate in the art and sex marketplaces as either artist or whore is to be at once both women, and the baby too. You are called to sacrifice yourself, or that which you hold dearest; you do things that were previously unimaginable to you; you are at different times exalted and exploited; and your ambitions, once ambient, crystallize viciously both in and out of reach. Getting what you want means giving something up; every solution is beautiful, violent.

On Fantasy

The first person who bought my art was a client of mine. Go figure. I sent him the auction link when it went live, and after a few hours he texted me saying that he was "the official owner" of my work. "Hot," I wrote back. I wanted him to buy it, knowing that to have been sold would make my work more salable writ large, and so I implied I'd take his buying the work as payment for the next time we saw one another.

The next time we saw one another, though, he still paid me, and I didn't say anything. I was glad. The show's curators got half the money from the sale of the work, and though my half still totaled more than he'd usually pay me for a single evening, I didn't want to feel like I was working off their half, which I implicitly would have been. I didn't want them to get any of my dirty money. They didn't need it, and neither did my client. Only I needed it.

I like this client; sometimes I fantasize about him. He fucked me on the bathroom floor once, and the next day my back was bruised. My friend and I see him together, and I have wild fantasies that he prefers her to me—eliciting horror, jealousy, and a kind of pure and twisted desire within me—which function to sustain my interest in him over an extended period of time.

I fawn over the idea of being collected, which is different from being owned. It is possession stemming from certain desirable characteristics, which might eclipse less desirable, or more complicated, characteristics at the moment of sale, but which are sure to show themselves to the collector over time. Does the collector then keep the overcomplicated object—with all its considerable maintenance, and finicky failures, and bratty displays of power? Does he grow to love the slow reveal of her imperfections, or does he disdain them? If he wishes to rid himself of her, how does he do so without regretting the entire investment—what psychological tricks must he play on himself to see her, still, as money well spent?

When her autofictional book *L'Inceste* was published, detailing her incestuous relationship with her father, Christine Angot was asked in an interview what she hoped to achieve from its publication. She answered, "My ambition is to be unmanageable. That people swallow me and at the same time cannot digest me." This is my most cherished fantasy.

Melissa Gira Grant defines her coined term *the prostitute imaginary* as "the ways in which we conceptualize and make arguments about prostitution . . . driven by both fantasies and fear about sex and the value of human life." For my part, I think there is a corresponding *artist imaginary*, driven by fantasies and fear about the value of human expression. Each imaginary centers around an irreconcilable conflict between fantasy and fear: the fantasy that something's price can or should correspond to its value as determined by the market's invisible hand, and then the fear that those matters of spirit that Judeo-Christian liberal capitalism teaches us are beyond the material world, including human life and expression—art, sex, love—are actually not beyond it, and can indeed be quantified or contained by its laws. The fantasy of capitalism as inevitable and rational collides with the fear that if it is, then anything—no matter how sacred—can indeed be bought and sold, with little fanfare.

I am a product of my environment. In their petite red-orange book, *Preliminary Materials for a Theory of the Young-Girl*, translated to English in 2011 as part of Semiotext(e)'s Intervention series, Tiqqun writes, "The world of the Young-Girl evinces a singular sophistication, in which reification has made added progress: In it, *human relations mask market relations which mask human relations* . . . Nothing is less personal than the 'personal value' of the Young-Girl." In the right context, the consumption of my body, and its attendant value, does not feel personal. There are two me's, and the me intentionally masking human relations with market relations is simply aggregating that experience into a particular track of my life, and, at times, bracketing it, so that the rest of my life feels less market-saturated. Perhaps this, too, though, is a fantasy: that I could effectively compartmentalize my own explicit commodification, making its edges neat so one *me* doesn't bleed onto the next. But at least it's *my* fantasy.

In 2002, eighty-five-year-old Leonora Carrington was profiled by the *New York Times*. At the time, Carrington was "one of the last surviving Surrealists," living in the same Mexico City townhouse she'd inhabited for over fifty years, replete with countless books, and her own art. The *Times* reported,

> It is all there in her paintings, an intimate, hermetic universe, where strange beings—half animal, half human—are involved in rituals of what seem to be profound metaphysical importance, all rendered in soft glowing tones that draw upon the techniques of the old masters. She resists talking about the sources for her work . . . But when pressed, she says softly . . . "I am as mysterious to myself as I am mysterious to others."

Fantasy—fantastical imagery—is central to Surrealism; Carrington is a master. In *Self-Portrait* (1937–38), she sits with her hand outstretched to a hyena whose breasts are swollen; a rocking horse floats behind them, untethered. I love this painting because—ever narcissistic—I see myself in it; her hair is dark and wild, like mine when I wake up, and her grasp on reality seems willingly slim, malleable, like anyone who spends a lot of time in their own head. Carrington maintains mystery, knowing mystery is the entry point for fantasy.

In their seminal work of affect theory, *Cruel Optimism*, Lauren Berlant writes, "Fantasy is the means by which people hoard idealizing theories and tableaux about how they and the world 'add up to something.'" Fantasy encompasses, manifests as, many other affective states, pleasurable and painful alike: lust, delusion, wonder, horror, longing, fear. Through the labors of sex and the labors of art—and each attendant marketplace—I have developed an intimate relationship with fantasy. I use it; I distrust it; I know it well; I am seduced by it; I should know better; I do not.

At twenty, Carrington met and fell in love with Max Ernst, then forty-six. She was young, beautiful, wild—Ernst called her his "bride of the wind." Most of the well-known Surrealists were men; she was a muse to them first, an artist in her own right second, at least to the outside world, though she wouldn't acquiesce to that order in her own telling. She was enveloped in fantasy; she was mired in it and she wielded it sharply and effectively in her writing and art; she also had a psychotic break and was institutionalized. A few years in, she was released to be sent to another sanatorium—but she escaped, living free thereafter.

Fantasy—and the sense of mystery that propels ardent belief in it—is central to the projects of selling art and selling sex.

Both markets prey on the universal desire for vigor, newness, intoxication, and a peculiarly earth-shifting—simultaneously immaterial and tactile—beauty. It's not to say these things that we buy and sell, acting as vessels to these states of being, are solely manufactured—they can be, but there is a basis of holy beauty to sex and to art that is *then* bought and sold. The holiness precedes the packaging. The packaging sometimes obscures the holiness.

In his first interview upon becoming editor-in-chief of *Artforum*, the leading contemporary art criticism magazine since 1962, David Velasco said,

> Art or whatever I call art, exceeds any sort of like . . . it's more important than my life. I could imagine actually sacrificing myself for a work of incredible art . . . which is yoked to a deeply stupid romanticism. I don't mean stupid in that I'm stupid. But the romance is dumb. It's feeling, and it spars with your rational brain, or simply smothers it. I think that a conviction in the affective powers of art to move, exhort, whatever, matched with a desire to articulate why that is, will be enough to keep us going.

When I am in a particular mood, when I want to be fucked a particular way, when it is just turning to spring, and the evening light is holding on, and I feel soft and sharp simultaneously—when these are the conditions, and I see a particularly beautiful person, I have an equally dumb thought: *I would probably let them do anything they wanted to me.*

Art and sex, then, and the pained and pleasured fantasies spun around them, each have the power—possibly the unique power—to make one feel such a way: willingly, gorgeously, carefully annihilated.

~

In the introduction to the Winter 2012 issue of *The Drama Review*—an issue dedicated to the topics of precarity and performance—Nicholas Ridout and Rebecca Schneider write, "The manipulation of affect is stock-in-trade for theatrical and performance labor, and much art production in general, in a post-Fordist economy driven . . . by the manufacture of affects as commodities. If affect is constitutively relational—or between bodies—how might it be understood as social and political? Are we living in the affect factory?" I, for one, am certainly *working* in the affect factory.

In 2021, I collapsed all of my identities onto themselves. Previously, I had written under my legal name—essays and reviews—unless I wrote about sex work, in which case I published under one or two pseudonyms. I solicited clients and created a public-facing escort persona, social media and all, under an entirely different name, and referred to myself as such with people who hired me. I had a whole other name to reveal to them as my real name—also fake—if they pushed too hard.

I was never very good at convincingly committing to multiple identities, or maybe it's more accurate to say that I was lazy about it. My efforts at promoting and becoming the me's without my real name were halfhearted, and it showed. Slowly, I thought, why not remain Sophia, full-time? I became myself and I quickly developed a higher retention rate with men who wanted to pay to sleep with me. Everyone preferred Sophia, which is to say: what people really want to buy from sex workers is not sex, but a mode of authenticity with fewer imperfections, and it was easier for me to feign this when I was pretending about other things less. I will always answer more warmly—more truly—to my own name.

The art and sex markets are ripe for scam—for price gouging and asset manipulation—because consumers are purchasing a conduit to a feeling. Each buyer is in search of a particular state of being and wants to see that state reflected back to themselves. Whether meaningful or shallow, the particular state one desires is priceless, as in: ever fervently and desperately sought, intrinsic to desire itself, commanding at whatever level of the market one is dipping into. The buyer is seeking confirmation of who they are, or who they want to be, or who they were, in purchasing a painting, or an overnight: a virile man; a widow with taste; a just-promoted banker; a cheating spouse; maybe a failson who wants, violently, success. I spoke with Sarah Michelson, a choreographer, about this phenomenon in a series of conversations in the summer of 2021. She assigned gestures to these ego relations, getting at the core of it. "Also like, what's driving sex work?" she asked. "In the gendered version of it. I guess it's ego related, you know, as we said before—'I'm throwing down my car key, I'm throwing down my wallet.'" I answered her, "Right, those embodied actions that reflect back to yourself who you are, what kind of man you see yourself as. The way these gendered gestures build our selves for our selves: 'I'm okay. This is what I'm doing, this is who I am.'" As a salesgirl and as a worker, I am able to produce these feelings for people more easily under my own name. This means I can make more money.

In 1974, Carlos Ginzburg staged a performance in Belgium, the photographic record of which would be called *Latin American Prostitute*. He negotiated with an Antwerp pimp who hired him out an Argentinian woman, reasoning that she was from his own country of origin. Ginzburg sat her in a gallery, holding a white sign with dark letters, reading, in French, "What is art? Prostitution." This is a quote from Charles Baudelaire's private journals; in the same passage, he writes, "Love is the desire to prostitute oneself. There is, indeed, no exalted pleasure which cannot be related to prostitution." By *prostitute oneself* he appears to mean to lay oneself bare; the definition seems less to do with money and more to do with a state of romantic, or ecstatic, abjection—to throw yourself at the feet of your beloved.

Of the piece, Ginzburg explains, "Of course it was a pure fiction; prostitutes are not working in museums with Baudelaire's quotation. But also it was not a fiction, and she was practicing prostitution. This total indetermination of the situation was very disturbing for everybody because there was the intuition and feeling she was doing real prostitution." Prostitutes are working in museums though, and I say this with the confidence of a person who knows and sees that prostitutes are working everywhere. According to art history scholar Julia Bryan-Wilson, "The woman was paid somewhat less than her usual fee for an afternoon's work" for executing Ginzburg's piece. I wonder why she was paid less, and why her pimp would agree to a discount—perhaps he was interested in the cachet of the art world? Bryan-Wilson adds, "It was rumored that she and a few male gallery-goers exchanged phone numbers and made dates for later."

That a prostitute exchanging phone numbers with male gallery-goers qualifies as a rumor implies there is something surprising or unlikely about such an exchange. Since this is an aspect of the prostitute's job—a simple and mundane transfer of information—what is surprising or unlikely, then, must be that she is doing her job in this setting, rather than offering up her visage as someone else's silent commentary on her job. It also seems to add frisson to the fact that men in this respectable setting are interested in her services. Such positioning—finding a respectable reason to enter a monied institution, and a way to slyly reveal what one does for a living, offering others a cover on how to talk to her about it—is familiar to prostitutes. I'd like to imagine the woman in Ginzburg's piece using the opportunity to make appointments her pimp might not know about, from which she could keep all the money. Men got to talk to her through the cover of engaging with an artwork, but of course what they really wanted was her; they always do. Ginzburg describing this framework as a "total indetermination" that was "very disturbing for everybody" belies the fact that what is happening is quite common and exceedingly decipherable. The inability to determine it is willful, for those who don't want to know what's going on or for some reason can't.

The willful confusion that is so easily generated by placing a whore in a different context than one expects to see her in remains a commonplace, pseudo-intellectual trick today. At a 2020 roundtable for the magazine *Sublevel*, the writer and pornographer Lorelei Lee criticized a frequent practice:

> It happens pretty often that artists, or writers, or documentary filmmakers, will want to make pornography their subject. They'll come to set and they'll frame the same photograph that the production assistant was just framing, or they'll take a shittier photograph behind the cameraperson who is actually creating pornography. It's like our performance is being viewed through the lens of someone who's socially sanctioned as an "artmaker" [which] gives the general public permission to find meaning in pornography as a subject, but without centering the voices of people who are actually making pornography and losing social credibility for making those performances.

An artist comes in, and suddenly everything is not as it was: this veil of willful confusion—this affective state called forth by a respectable artist's participation in an unrespectable aesthetic or event—has a sharp, and often cruel, edge. The whore is stripped of her intellect, as though she couldn't possibly be smart enough to create her own commentary on what her presence within a gatekept institution might signify.

A friend wrote an article for a legacy publication on the rampant popularity of the porn site OnlyFans; the photographer for the magazine asked to photograph content creators at work, and then complained to my friend—as though astonished—when the creators told him, "No, you cannot shoot us at work, because what you will be shooting, then, is porn, which your magazine will not accept." Upon final review of the piece, the standards department questioned her use of the phrase "jerk-off instruction (JOI)" in the opening paragraph. She lamented: "What exactly am I supposed to say? You hired me to write about porn and then you don't want me to write about porn."

The women profiled for the piece received, essentially, free advertising in the form of sultry photographs in the pages of a nationally read magazine, the photographs—licensed from their social media and fan pages—cropped so as not to appear truly pornographic, but suggesting the reveal of a naked body, or the presence of a strap-on. I would imagine they encountered an influx of new subscribers. I would also imagine that they were contacted by an influx of men explaining why they did not want to subscribe or otherwise purchase the services of a sex worker, but instead wanted to engage in conversation about what was said in the piece, if the women would be so kind as to indulge them. This willful confusion, then, beyond erasing the intellect of sex workers, so too allows voyeurs and reticent client-types to engage sex workers as not-quite-sex-workers, allows them to act as though there might be any reason to fulfill their fantasies—discursive or not—for free.

After I collapsed all of my disparate identities into one, someone wrote to me: "I came across your website and I read some of your writing. You are so provocative and potentially irresistible. But, alas, your rates are so high." I don't know what possessed me to respond to such a whiny lament, but I did—I think because I no longer have rates listed anywhere and wanted to know what he was referring to. I replied, saying as much, and suggested he send a gift to signal his appreciation of my work, if he couldn't afford to spend time with me. I hadn't realized, but the same person had inquired about my rates months earlier, and that was how he knew. He wrote back, "You had responded a few months ago with your rate. Thanks for the idea of sending a gift, though it might not be overly orgasmic for me (though it's better to give than to receive, of course)." This is the kind of person who enjoys willful confusion: someone who detests the idea of paying for your time; someone who thinks a firm price is applicable to others but not him, never him; someone who sees nothing you do as work.

In another text—*Desire/Love*—Lauren Berlant writes of desire, promise, and drama: "Desire describes a state of attachment to something or someone, and the cloud of possibility that is generated by the gap between an object's specificity and the needs and promises projected onto it . . . Your style of addressing those objects gives shape to the drama with which they allow you to reencounter yourself." In the United States, the *promise* of heterosexual, penetrative sex is projected onto the prostitute insofar as she cannot overtly advertise it. What is precisely illegal is to promise sex in exchange for something. The discursive moment is the crime. So long as the promise remains a projection, she has broken no laws. In her essay "Calling My Work What It Is," Charlotte Shane writes, "I believe the difference between 'escort' and 'prostitute' is that one term relies on euphemistic window dressing while the other is unapologetic and unashamed. It's usually bracketed by large amounts of clothed or non-physical time, but I sell the promise of heterosexual, penetrative sex." Shane alights on a key facet of marketing: the sale of a promise.

So the "cloud of possibility" blooms through imagery that suggests but does not prescribe. The high-end (read: expensive; often in class drag) escort advertises herself through a gallery of images on her website. She might not show her face or her pussy, but there will more than likely appear a bare breast and nipple; a suggestion of pubic hair (unless she advertises as barely nineteen, in which case, her skin will be smooth and naked); an arched foot; an arched back; freshly blown-out hair; Facetune-ed nose, cheeks, and forehead; a manicured finger somewhere near her mouth.

In one photo she might wear Calvins, promising an authentic closeness, a casual intimacy that, the buyer likes to think, can't be bought; he has to believe the possibility to be there, but only if (he vainly hopes) their chemistry is real, her desire true. Tiqqun writes, "It appears that all of the concreteness of the world has taken refuge in the ass of the Young-Girl," and this is what the client feels when he looks at her image in a cotton thong. In another, she wears a full Agent Provocateur set with Wolford thigh-highs and Louboutin heels with their Crayola-red soles—like a matte lipstick accidentally made glossy—promising luxury. Luxury in the context of sex is oxymoronic, as luxury relies on trappings, and good sex is fast to rid itself of trappings, but nonetheless, these photos signify at the very least a particular atmosphere saturated with money. A naked body adorned with accessories so expensive and so impractical promises a sound investment and a commitment to the fantasy. In another, the escort wears a designer dress appropriate for a muted evening out; in another, a silk slip, hair falling in front of her face; in another, nothing at all, her back to us, looking down at a city from a great height in an expansive hotel room. So the promise is heterosexual sex, yes; but the promise is also the window dressing. The window dressing might be what's wanted most of all: the way the promise of sex, and the build-up to it—particularly the build-up to new sex—makes you feel.

In his memoir detailing his experience of heroin addiction, Michael Clune describes the idea of *the first time* in a way that's always stuck with me: "There's a little rip in my brain when I look at a white-topped vial. The rip goes deep, right down to the bone, to the very first time. People love whatever's new. Humans love the first time. The first time is life. Life is always fading. The work of art is to make things new. The work of advertising is to make things new." Good art, good sex, and good market advertising for both promise the feeling of the first time. Life *is* always fading; it's certainly fading for most of the clients I've ever met. The rote copy on escort sites is nonetheless seductive, dangling the rush of anticipation, meeting, succumbing—even if it's been promised countless times, the promise never gets old.

I met a client who described his fantasy as the following: the first time a girl falls into his arms in a hotel room, as soon as she walks through the door. When I went to see him, I knocked, and immediately he pulled me into his arms and stuck his tongue in my mouth. I remained in his embrace in the half-closed doorframe as long as I could, but I desperately had to pee, and when I inevitably broke the kiss, he apologized: "I'm sorry, I was just sticking with the fantasy." "I know," I said, "I just really have to pee." The not-knowing-me—the mystery—allowed the fantasy to take shape; my specificity was important only insofar as it could be mapped onto the desired scene. I was a proxy for the first-time-falling-girl; any number of women could have been her, but in that moment, it was me. In her work on the function of the "proxy" within digital image-making—the unreality of the digital images we produce—artist and theorist Hito Steyerl writes of "smartphone camera technology":

> The lenses are tiny and basically rubbish, which means that about half of the data being captured by the camera sensor is actually noise. The trick, then, is to write the algorithm to . . . discern the picture from inside the noise . . . It scans all other pictures stored on the phone or on your social media networks . . . It analyzes the pictures you already took . . . and tries to match faces and shapes to link them back to you. By comparing what you and your network already photographed, the algorithm guesses what you might have wanted to photograph now. It creates the present picture based on earlier pictures, based on your/its memory. The result might be a picture of something that never ever existed, but that the algorithm thinks you might like to see.

This is the peculiarity of what the sex worker sells: an expanse of lovely noise and minimal information, easily—sometimes unconsciously—sifted through to turn up something *you might like to see.* A blankness with just enough particularity to become a dream fulfillment; a signifier to match what has already been signified; someone simultaneously invisible and without substitute.

Another time, I met someone who wrote me an email afterward recounting our time together, beginning with our first kiss, in which he described himself as trembling with desire, whereas I perceived shaking with nervousness. Are they really so different? Outside of the thrall of desire, I observe these bodily interactions at a remove, with—internally—cold indifference. In the thrall—in the drama—he reencounters himself through me, through accessing the generative function of his own desire, through access to me. To me, he sweats and squirms; to him, life bursts through.

I watched *The Sopranos* during my first years escorting. I spent hours upon hours lying in bed, making my way through the six seasons, simultaneously checking my email and editing photos on my phone. It is, arguably, my favorite work of art. I bought a Sopranos baseball cap with the name of Tony's strip club, Bada Bing, embroidered across the front. I posted a photo of myself wearing the cap and a tight denim bodysuit to my work Twitter, captioning it "Cosplaying Adriana." At some point, a man whose Twitter handle included the name David Chase wrote to me, and I thought, *If only.*

In a third-season episode, Carmela—mob wife—views a painting at the Met that brings her to tears: *The Holy Family with Saints Anne and Catherine of Alexandria*, completed in 1648 by Jusepe de Ribera. The painting depicts Saint Catherine's mystical marriage to Christ, who is shown as the baby Jesus; Carmela's daughter, Meadow, scoffs, "She's marrying a baby? Good luck," to which Carmela responds, in a murmur, "We all do." Through the painting, Carmela reencounters herself and the gap between her choices and those of Saint Catherine: she is married to a man who is in many respects monstrous; she reaps the financial rewards of organized crime—theft and murder—hoping that performative churchgoing and confession will wash her hands of sin. She longs for a purity of soul that she long ago gave up in exchange for nice things. She wants a return to the first time—and its possibilities—in the deepest way: a clean slate, a resurrection, a mystical marriage untainted by all the violent impurities of her world that have become horrifyingly mundane. The art rends her open in a way nothing else has, or can; she reencounters herself before the painting, and she weeps.

Later in the same episode, Carmela's husband, Tony—mob boss—laments to his therapist about the volatile nature of his current extramarital affair with a woman named Gloria: "Me and this broad, we're like leather and lace, a burning ring of fire . . . Whatever the fuck." She offers in response, "Amour fou, as the French call it. Crazy love, all-consuming." This is what affairs offer: an irrational pull; a lust or fullness of desire that both highlights and obscures other realities of one's life. Tony's drama with Gloria rends him open: he wants the object he wants, in spite of, or probably because of, its surety to end in flames; he reencounters himself through his serial affairs, and he blusters, and threatens violence, and exposes tenderness.

These modes of reencountering—these objects of desire—are gendered. Carmela gets art; Tony gets sex. I, for one, want both—and there were times I thought I could have both only through embodiment; that the surest defense against losing access to either was to *be* sex and to *be* art—for the consumption of others, and for the reassurance of myself that I was bound up with what I wanted. But sometimes to be inside something is to be very far from it.

I met someone when I was first starting out. We matched on Tinder; she was looking for a girl to play with her and her sugar daddy. We got frozen margaritas at a bar with picnic tables in its backyard, and as we huddled at one in the corner, she told me what their meetings were like, what he liked. I wasn't sure if we were on a date or simply discussing work, which is how a lot of sex worker meet-ups go—flirting under the guise of advice-giving or collegial story-trading. I was too nervous to go forward with the work, and texted her that I wasn't ready, but that I really appreciated her time. It was true; I did. She gave me excellent tips: try to avoid clients with tech money, if you can, since they're the best at stalking; only work for married guys, since they have the least free time and the most to lose from outing you.

We followed one another peripherally on Instagram, and a few years on—I was now reasonably well-versed at working on my own—she posted a call to friends in the industry for participation in a scene, in coded language: "I have a work opportunity! DM me, if you know you know [winky face]." I wrote to her, saying I'd love to work together, if she was still looking. She instructed me to dress "girl next door."

I arrived at her house, along with two other workers. We sipped tequila as she debriefed us on the scene ahead: her client liked to play out the same fantasy every time, with a rotating group of people that always included her. He was a legendary character; apparently, he had been passed down among an unbroken line of queer sex workers for decades, his scene requirements never changing, even minutely. We were to play-act virgins—friends of hers from the college she told him she went to—who had never touched a dick before. He would teach us how to give a hand job and, for extra money, a blow job. Coming of age during the onset of AIDS, he was fanatical about safe sex and used condoms even for hand-to-genital contact.

The client was kind. It seemed his greatest fantasy was to be a teacher of virgins, to open a school for non-wayward girls. He told us how his dick would react when he ejaculated, so that we wouldn't be surprised. At a certain point, he was blindfolded, allowing us to make faces at one another; we laughed silently, exaggeratedly miming shock and awe as the lessons became more scientific, more absurd. I saw him with her a few times, with a few different friends. It was easy and silly. His fantasy was so powerful that the scene appeared fully new for him every time, regardless of repeated involvement—there was no acknowledgment that he'd met me before. He wanted me to be an unknown virgin, and so I was.

On one occasion, it happened that his mother had died earlier that day. He took a call from his adult child in the middle of the session, comforting her. I was surprised he wanted to keep the date, having lost a parent, but grief is a strange bird, and really, I knew nothing about him. That time, our play took on a level of care, at least in my mind; I wanted to be kind back to him, and to imbue the scene with some sort of genuine delight. I was extra playful and warm, laughing at his jokes easily and kissing his chest.

As my friend and I—another friend, one whom I'd had sex with before but only in the context of work, rubbing our pussies together for a young hedge fund guy who could barely stay hard—traded his dick back and forth, pretending we could hardly stretch our mouths around it, and theatrically choking, egging each other on, I thought about everyone who had been in my position before. I marveled at the power of a fantasy that never gets old, the kind that functions as the one true desire. To be in thrall to a fantasy like this seems like a work of art to me: there is a purity to it, and a trueness. He was true to his fantasy. He did not deviate. It had a nearly divine hold over him.

I wondered if his virgin fantasy had anything to do with his mother; if the loss of her was also the loss of the origin of his sexual desires, or if the two were in his mind entirely apart. I wondered if death was kinky to him. I felt both a responsibility that I would always feel in the presence of a person mourning, and some kind of judgment about why he wanted to be there in the midst of grieving. Or perhaps my judgment was of his fantasy—his need for it so profound it overruled all else. I felt flickers of disdain for him for wanting this on the day of his mother's death, because I feared being a person who could someday want such a thing, on such a day, too, and what that would reflect about the lonely conditions of my life. But I also felt a relief that he didn't cancel, because I was expecting a certain amount of money that night, and I wanted to walk away with it as I'd intended. It was dissonant to be in the presence of someone for whom sex and death were, in that moment, impossibly close, while neither were immediately present for me, not even sex; though I was an active and integral participant, to me, this wasn't sex, but work.

Another time, as he handed us our wads of cash and descended the stairs to the basement-level bathroom, he warned, "Now don't start doing this a lot, don't become *prostitutes* or anything." We laughed uneasily; one of us made a motion to reassure him. "I know *this* money seems fast and fun, but *that's* not," he said, expressing an even more deeply held fantasy: more than virgins, we categorically *weren't hookers*. He needed to believe in a demarcation between what he hired us to do and what other men might hire us to do, and also to believe we wouldn't let ourselves be hired, and ruined, by those other men. For the sanctity of his fantasy, we could only be his.

Maggie Nelson writes,

> Imagine, for example, someone who fucks like a whore. Someone who seems good at it, professional. Someone you can still see fucking you, in the mirror, always in the mirror . . . in an apartment lit by blue light, never lit by daylight, this person is always fucking you from behind in blue light and you both always seem good at it . . . as if there is no other activity on God's given earth your bodies know how to do except fuck and be fucked like this, in this dim blue light, in this mirror. What do you call someone who fucks this way?

An artist, I think.

Nelson writes this in *Bluets*, her meditation on the color blue. I read *Bluets* in my boyfriend's farmhouse one summer; I figured it was time to read Nelson, and the book was slim and thus approachable. I was surprised that, among every blue thing she mentioned, and among every reference to the body and lust and violence, she failed to name steak cooked blue—that is, just seared on the outside, all but untouched by heat on the inside. Steak is like sex, is like art: bloody; gets you high; is disgusting if you think about it for too long. And blue steak, then, is like sex work: a carefully crafted artifice that allows for the presentation of something ostensibly raw to the consumer, without the risks of actual raw consumption. The person who orders blue steak feels it as real, and animal, though it is sanitized, and carefully so.

In SoHo, there is a boutique hotel whose rooms are blue. Blue carpet, blue ceiling, blue-patterned sheets. I met a client there several years ago, when I still had short bangs. I wore a vintage skirt and top set—black, with colorful flowers—and black lingerie from l'Agent, the now-defunct, less expensive little sister brand to Agent Provocateur. My client wanted our time together to feel like a movie. He didn't say this, but his behavior made it clear. He booked me for only an hour but wanted an experiential arc: he sat me first in the small living room area of his suite, presenting liquor he had put on ice for me. Music played softly through the room's sound system: "Nothing's Gonna Hurt You Baby" by Cigarettes After Sex, a song that I'd only ever heard as the background of a bad television show. He moved me into the bedroom, bantering, as though he had to charm me. I have absolutely no recollection of what he looked like or what his name was. This isn't because I was seeing so many clients I couldn't keep track, but because it's useless information to retain after the fact. I remember how he behaved—the only salient thing—which was annoying, and also standard, fine. I overstayed our appointment because the sex refused to end, as happens often with older men who want to paw at a young woman but don't quite care whether or not they finish, and certainly not in the allotted time. "Nothing's Gonna Hurt You Baby" returned to the playlist; it was looping, as was the experience.

I played the song for myself after, alone in my own room. A user called "i'm cyborg but that's ok" had uploaded it to YouTube along with a compilation of scenes from *Lost in Translation*, a movie I'd never seen but that I knew was about a relationship between a washed-up older man having a midlife crisis and a beautiful young woman. The video compilation looked like an escort advertisement: in the opening scene, Scarlett Johansson sits in a hotel room window wearing only a large men's shirt—blue—looking down at the wide expanse of Tokyo beneath her; in the next cut scene, she dives into an enormous, empty hotel pool, at night—the pool and the surrounding windowpanes all blue, too. The images spoke of money and alienation. The song captured the affect of a certain type of client: slightly flat; grasping toward a Daddy-esque certainty but falling short; single-mindedly offering reassurance, but of what he hardly seemed to know. I grew oddly attached to the song and cyborg's music video for a period. I would watch it on my way to work, flattening my own affect, compacting myself into a version of a girl aligned with the lyrics:

> Whispered something in your ear
> It was a perverted thing to say
> But I said it anyway
> Made you smile and look away
> Nothing's gonna hurt you, baby.

I've still never seen *Lost in Translation*, but it came up again during a duo a few months ago, when my friend bantered with our shared client about favorite films, while I pretended to keep up. She said she felt hateful saying so, but that she bought into the rumor that it was Sofia Coppola's boyfriend at the time, Spike Jonze, who really directed the film, because when they broke up, her work went immediately downhill. Leaning in, my friend made us swear we'd never repeat her secret belief. Our client laughed and put one hand on each of our legs, the part that is somehow both knee and thigh. I smiled placidly, sipping wine. Later he, too, failed to finish in the allotted time, but, blessedly, he ended the sex anyway of his own volition. He said, "Enough," and briefly took us to his chest, before stepping away and counting our money. Afterward, my friend, new to the work, was surprised: "I can't believe he didn't come?" We walked down the street holding hands. "It's common," I told her, "and usually more annoying than that."

A couple years after my first visit, I returned to the blue hotel, seeing a different client. I wore a mini schoolgirl skirt, which he remarked on favorably. When I met him in the hotel lobby—the elevator required a key card after a certain hour—he said to me, "I think about you all the time." It was the first time he said it, though I'd been seeing him for months, and it was the first time I would have believed it, too. He said it almost by accident, which is a way to discern the truth. This client knew who I was: knew my legal name and, therefore, true aspects of my life. I know who he is, and who his wife is, and where he works and lives, who his friends and his boss are. For the duration of the time I saw him—somewhere between six months and a year—he claimed to fear, above all, his wife discovering his infidelities and the subsequent destruction of his domestic life, but his behavior suggested otherwise. He was reckless with information and found me not on an escort ad site but a sugar dating site, where men who want or need to pay for sex, for one reason or another, but are reticent to do so, look for women who are willing to sell sex while pretending, adamantly, that they are not professionals, and that no exchange of labor for money is taking place.

This is a different pretending than the pretending that is still legally necessary within straightforward prostitution, where (good) client and prostitute conspire together to communicate in such a way that it could conceivably appear to any interested law enforcement parties that—as the disclaimers on most escort sites read—"money exchanged is for time and companionship only," and "anything that happens during that time is a matter of privacy between two consenting adults and has not been contracted for nor compensated." I think implicit in this contract—the unspoken contract between client and escort—is professional discretion, but only insofar as the client understands he is hiring a professional, for a service. If, instead, you find a girl on a sugar dating site, and if you insist that she is not a professional you are hiring—which then requires all kinds of affective labor on her part to make this feel true—it follows that she should not, then, be held to professional standards of discretion and secrecy. It would be so much wiser for men in need of discretion to strictly hire, rather than sugar date, but many are too proud to explicitly acknowledge the labor involved in seeing them. It never ceases to amaze me what men are willing to risk to protect their own egos.

The point is, I could ruin his life. Easily. I won't though, not out of loyalty to him, necessarily, but because I simply have no interest in doing so. I think he had an interest in me doing so; I think it might have been his greatest fantasy. The second time we met, his wife was away, and we spent the night together. I was still feeling out how high I could set my rates and insisted on a bonus fee when he asked me beforehand, over text, to shave my pubic hair. I had never shaved all of my pubic hair off before—the most I'd done was a landing strip—and it had always seemed a bit impossible to me. The kind of thing other, more aesthetically perfect girls do, that I could never do. I did it, though, because I was paid to, and it wasn't as difficult as it seemed. Afterward, bare, I thought I looked amphibian-like, and years younger. I was embarrassed when I fucked my boyfriend; I took my underwear off to show him but kept my shirt on, which made me look even more naked than fully nude.

This client also wanted our time together to be cinematic. I suppose all clients do. The first time we met, I was struck by his impulse to narrate what was happening, as though by speaking aloud how good something is one could will it to actually be so. It's not that it wasn't good, or was bad—it was just mundane, the way formulaic excess often is. He loved cocaine, and he liked to inhale it off my body, and wanted me to do the same. He seemed to want to be in a party scene from *The Wolf of Wall Street*; a nearly prescriptive commitment to hedonism turned him on. He was also frightened by this fantasy, though that fear was blunted, a bit, by the drugs.

That first time, he took a phone call in the bathroom, and then peeked out from behind the half-ajar door, mouthing to me with his hand over the mouthpiece, "I just like watching you," while I stretched and smiled, offering myself up through studied pose to be seen as beatific, natural, relaxed. Our afternoon was peppered by comments like that, observations of what he wanted to be so, not necessarily what strictly *was* so: "I'm with a hot girl in a hotel room in the middle of the day, drinking champagne, how did I get so lucky"; "Look at us, I'm doing lines off your perfect ass"; "I feel so comfortable with you, like we've known each other forever." It didn't matter that he wasn't lucky, he was just rich; it didn't matter whether or not my ass was perfect, because perfection is in the eye of the beholder; and it didn't matter that he felt comfortable only because I made sure that he did, receiving every stray thought and confession with warmth, or laughter, or a doe-eyed openness. He talked himself into believing it was all happenstance, fate.

The next time, high and glassy-eyed, close to my face, he whispered, "I can trust you, right?" "Yes," I answered, "of course." He wanted to open up the world to me, and so I pretended my world had been closed before him. "You have no idea how beautiful you are, do you?" he asked, while undressing me. "No man has ever cared about your pleasure like this, has he," while he spun his fingers around inside me, an unwieldy carousel of self-validation and drug-addled clumsiness. He brought me to his home that night, under the guise of wanting to show me a book he had there. We took a cab, and he insisted on rolling the windows down even though it was winter, "because of Covid," which I found absurdly funny—the idea of any kind of risk mitigation while taking a stranger to one's home that one shares, monogamously, with one's wife, in a pandemic. In the cab, he used his phone to disable their security cameras. Once at their place, he showed me the book—like an afterthought, or a forethought to rush through as a necessity before getting to what he really wanted to do—and then gave me a tour. His apartment was beautiful; I didn't like being there. We reached the master bathroom and he pushed me against the mirror, bringing my hand to his belt buckle. I left him for a moment, to find my bag and get a condom out of it, and when I returned, he fucked me over the sink. I noticed his wife's clothes in the laundry hamper and, after, the books on her side of the bed, and felt not quite guilty but astonished by his betrayal, which I was witness to.

As we continued to see one another with increasing regularity—as the months went on—we began a dance, wherein he acknowledged himself as a client, but only insofar as he was unavailable to be a boyfriend because of his marriage. I gave him the impression that were it not for his wife, I would date him for free; that he paid me, essentially, to make up for the fact that he could not date me, that the relationship was on his terms and his timeline, and that I expressed no emotional needs, save for the ones he wanted me to, to stoke his conception of himself as a sensitive guy. I told him as much in a hotel known for its clawfoot tubs; we passed bubbles back and forth and listened to a bad Spotify playlist, and it was, all things considered, easy and nice. He left to meet his family for dinner and I took Polaroids of myself on the bed, by the tub, in white lace underwear and with my dress half-buttoned. I wanted to document myself as I was then: unkempt and paid, but for what, exactly? For becoming that person, that particular version, for him, on a Friday afternoon.

The next time I saw him was in the blue room. It was different than I remembered; brighter, but also emptier, rid of a minibar due to pandemic restrictions. He did fuck me from behind, in front of the mirror, and he mimed Christian Bale's choreography in *American Psycho*, which alarmed me, given that Bale murders the sex workers he fucks. But I think my client's mimicry was still more to do with the unbridled wealth of Bale's character, rather than his killer tendencies; he was intoxicated by the money and the social dominance it gave him. Bale sees no difference between these girls and the blue steak; my client, I believe, did. Nonetheless, he often joked that if I told his wife, he'd have to kill me. "I'd like to see you try," I always wanted to say, but instead I would laugh, as though the threat was funny, rather than sick.

An hour into our meeting, I remembered that an application for an arts residency was due before midnight that night and I leapt up, surprised by my transposing of dates I'd checked several times, determined not to let the possibility of guaranteed studio space slip away. I cocooned myself in an armchair, ten feet from the bed, promising I'd be no more than a half hour. I broke character for the first time, taking myself off the clock and tending fully to the tedium of uploading documents, made harder by the absence of a computer. "Could you do your typing with your other hand on my cock," he half whined. Where usually I'd relent, I said no without so much as a raised eyebrow, too distracted to placate him. The spell burst, but, still, with only us in the room, nothing could rush in to replace it but a slightly different version: no choice but to see me as his studious part-time girlfriend, his aspiring artist—or else admit our circumstances to be little more than an elaborate joke. He had no ground to stand on to refuse me.

Later, he kissed me in front of a second mirror, thrusting the bitter taste of cocaine into my mouth, and then directed me downward. "Look how hard you get me," he said, "no one gets me this hard." He said it as though I hadn't noticed him take a pill out of his bag and pop it, as though his erection was proof that all the money he'd spent on me to that point was worth it: tens of thousands of dollars so that we might mutually make believe a manufactured blood flow was instead born of wild desire, desire only I could draw forth. That's what fucking like a whore—like an artist—is, doing the work to make us both seem good at it. There's no secret save for willful deception, bought into by both parties. An American dream.

Neither of us ever fired the other, but at a certain point, we stopped seeing each other. I wasn't working as much while I was writing, and he seemed to glean, accurately, that whatever fantasy I could offer him had worn thin. He was the first person that I saw over a long period of time whom I disclosed my identity to, which I did because of art world connections he offered, and because it would have ultimately been too inconvenient not to—he wanted it so badly. He was profoundly attached to an idea of me, and the more me I became, publicly, the less his idea could stay intact, like a favored T-shirt rendered unwearable, finally, with holes.

When I first began escorting, I also worked sporadically in a massage parlor, filling in for friends calling out of shifts, or picking up days when they were offered to me, last-minute.

The clientele were odd: largely men who wanted full-service companionship but, for one reason or another, were reluctant to hire a prostitute advertising as such. They sought massages instead—markedly cheaper—and negotiated for extras. I recall a man saying to me that he had tried hiring prostitutes, but he found the experience to be clinical, lacking in warmth. I wondered if the women he hired failed to touch him in places other than his cock. It's easy to forget to touch someone when the desire isn't there, just as it's difficult to stop touching a person—everywhere—when the desire is. I pet my boyfriend like I do our cat: on his head, on his back, on his arms, on his chest—anywhere exposed to me. Touch is an open channel; running your fingers gently over someone's skin, imbuing it with romantic but not sexual feeling, is one of the surest ways to foster intimacy. Perhaps these frugal daytime clients came for the promise of extended touch, a massage indicating that every aspect of the body would be tended to.

The massage parlor was the only time I've performed sex work with colleagues in the vicinity, where we were not tending to the same client. I've worked with others seeing the same client, together—a duo—but at the parlor, someone else was simply doing the same job in the other room. This made me feel safe and inspired a longing for an idealized communal place of sex work—really, a brothel. I loved the idea of gossiping with friends, waiting for a client to show up, as opposed to the alienating routine of getting ready and winding down in solitude.

A client came in once who was exceedingly good-looking: young and tall, with a sharply defined face. I was briefly turned on. Almost immediately, though, he grew repulsive to me, as it became evident he wanted penetrative sex without paying the going rate for it, and thus had found himself here, hoping someone might benevolently offer him a bargain. I felt annoyed and cheap, unsure if there would be a number I could upsell him to that would even make taking off my underwear worth it. We were in a room with no bed—just a massage table and a couch—and he crowded me on the table, pulling me from a sitting position so I was instead lying next to him, which there was no space for.

In the same year, in the same parlor, I saw an older white client. He engaged me in a conversation; I forget much of what we spoke about, but I think I pretended to be more literary than I was. I remember that he was a professorial type—condescending, liberal. He told me he liked coming to this parlor—which might more accurately be described as an apartment in an upscale neighborhood, housing two workers at a time on various shifts, who were, often, because of the milieu of the girls who ran the place, white and college-educated—because he felt like the girls here must like the work more. He imagined we all had other options for how we might make money, and had chosen this. He had been to other parlors, he said—and he didn't quite say the quiet part out loud, but it was implicit from the coded language he used that the workers at these other parlors were largely women of color, and that he actually knew nothing about their backgrounds, but had no awareness of this lack of knowledge—and he feared that the workers at those parlors were trafficked, at worst, or, at best, were there purely due to financial need, and were entirely sexually disinterested in him.

I was, of course, entirely sexually disinterested in him. I was also there of my own free will, and so he was right not to worry that I wasn't. And yet, all work that's done only because we need money feels coercive. When I told him I did full-service work, he hired me for an hour at a hotel, and though I could barely get through it because I was the most depressed

I had ever been, for reasons unrelated to work, and smiling was painful, and being touched was painful—I still did get through it because I needed to pay my rent. Of course I had options: I could have done something else; I could have worked longer hours at a different job; I wouldn't have been in dire straits had I been unable to pay my rent; I had parents and a partner and friends and a sibling who all would swiftly loan me money. But I went, and I easily fulfilled his fantasy that I wanted to be there—even though no one wants to be at work, most of the time—simply because I had the right combination of identities to appear carefree and willing as opposed to whatever he perceived as in acute need. He chose me for this outside work, and he happily paid me—revolted, bored, melancholy, quasi-suicidal as I was—because my whiteness and the upscale location of the massage parlor matched his fantasy.

This client's self-deception is the flipside of an insidious savior industry and savior complex that shadows the sex industry, feeding off of it like so many evangelizing, saccharinely violent leeches. While there are certainly overtly predatory clients, seeking the youngest and most vulnerable girls, there are also just as many clients fearful of encountering trafficked women, for myriad reasons: scared they'll be arrested; scared they'll be de facto morally responsible for rape; scared that sex with a trafficked worker reflects poorly on their sexual prowess or masculinity, that it means she *really* didn't want to do it. Trafficked workers in the United States—in every industry, including, for example, agriculture—are disproportionately non-white and non–US citizens, and so the state, rather than "rescuing" such workers into a better life, as it claims to do, continues to criminalize and brutalize them. moses moon (aka thotscholar)—author and self-described "erotic laborer" and "low end theorist"—writes,

> Women and girls of color, including the trafficking victims whom the criminalization of sex work purportedly "saves," are disproportionately targeted and criminalized by law enforcement, which fails to protect them from the racist and gendered violence they commonly experience while engaging in "survival sex" or other forms of sex work. Minors, particularly Black girls, are still being arrested on charges of prostitution in certain states and criminalized when they defend themselves against sexual violence.

The affective demand within the sex industry to convince a client that one is a willing participant in the work, as opposed to a coerced participant, is distributed unevenly across race. Which is to say, the demand falls squarely on non-white workers.

The dominant conception of consent within work, and particularly within sex work, is vastly oversimplified, built on a fantasy that there are simply those willingly working and those unwillingly working—or, in human trafficking language, those being sold—when in reality, the function of consent within sex work varies wildly from person to person and circumstance to circumstance, creating a gray, interpersonal tapestry of choice, force, autonomy, and oppression, all against a backdrop of capitalist state violence.

In 2017, thirty-eight-year-old Yang Song died during an NYPD vice raid on the massage parlor at which she worked in Flushing, Queens. Though the NYPD officially declared her death an accident or a suicide in a 2018 report, many hold the force responsible for murder, if indirectly. According to surveillance footage, Song jumped or fell four stories in an attempt to evade arrest, though she was still "listed as 'arrested' for violating, NYPL § 230.00 Prostitution, under arrest no. Q17652546"—listed as such, mind you, while dying in a hospital. The circumstances surrounding her death were unimaginably cruel. She was sexually assaulted during the last year of her life by a police officer who came to the parlor, flashed his badge, and demanded sexual services in return for refraining from arresting her—and Song had been arrested before, in a similar raid to the one precipitating her death. In the same documentation ruling her death a suicide or accident, the NYPD cited the following as "evidence of [her] criminality":

> Yang Song's conduct of removing IMOS-UC1 from the apartment when he would not remove his clothing as well as her subsequent response of pacing back and forth and observing the DVR monitor which provided a live feed of the field team approaching her apartment; and . . . Yang Song's criminal history which included previous arrests for prostitution at the same subject location.

Herein lies the deeply violent edge of fantasy: the NYPD fantasized that Song was a criminal and a prostitute, and thus crowded her into a position wherein she would have to behave as such. After deciding she was deserving of a raid, no possible behavior by her could then indicate non-criminality—going through with the appointment or cutting the appointment off could both fit neatly within the criminal-prostitute-fantasy narrative. Commitment to fantasy is embedded within the functioning of the carceral state; it is a vessel through which nearly any action by a person-fantasized-as-criminal can easily flow, turning the mundane to evidence like alchemy.

In the wake of Song's death, Red Canary Song, a Queens-based grassroots massage parlor worker coalition, formed to fight for justice and police accountability. In 2019, responding to the solicitation case brought against the billionaire Robert Kraft for patronizing an erotic massage parlor in Florida—

leading to sensationalized media claiming the massage workers were trafficked and enslaved—Red Canary Song wrote for *Tits and Sass*, a website providing "service journalism by and for sex workers":

> The public is fed the racist myth that all Chinese massage parlors are involved in human trafficking. In fact, most Chinese workers do this work because it is the most sensible work for them to do, especially when they are new immigrants to the country and do not have access to other opportunities or employment training. For many, it is simply the fastest way to send money home, and it makes the most practical sense at this time of their lives. "The massage parlor is a platform for our survival [here] when there are not [a lot] of other services to help immigrants transition into the country," explains Elle, a veteran Flushing massage parlor worker.

The very perception that certain forms of work, like massage parlor work, are by default sex work—regardless of what an individual is or isn't actually offering—as well as the fantasy that women in these circumstances are necessarily being trafficked, renders such workers vulnerable to interpersonal and state violence, both of which are frequently fatal. The Kraft case began as an investigation into human trafficking—meaning, ostensibly, the state would see the workers involved as victims, rather than criminals—but quickly morphed, as the workers were arraigned on prostitution charges, and the assistant state attorney announced, "There is no human trafficking that arises out of this investigation."

On March 16, 2021, Robert Aaron Long killed eight people in a mass shooting across three spas in Atlanta, Georgia. Six of the victims were Asian women who were massage parlor workers: Daoyou Feng, Hyun Jung Kim Grant, Soon Chung Park, Suncha Kim, Xiaojie Tan, and Yong Ae Yue. Long blamed his "sex addiction" for his actions, stating to the police that the parlors were a "temptation for him that he wanted to eliminate."

In a reported essay for *Vanity Fair* on the lives of the victims and survivors of the shootings, journalist May Jeong writes,

> The occupation [of spa work] is as common in immigrant communities as it is misunderstood. According to Georgia state human-trafficking awareness training, people with limited English skills living at their place of work is considered a sign of sex trafficking, yet these are standard practices among workers. The work itself might mean ordinary massages, or it might mean massages that include erotic services—specifically manual stimulation, which some workers do not think of as sex work, as it doesn't involve penetration. Workers like Kim can make as much as $20,000 in a good month. That money supports families in this country and the other.

Kim—Hyun Jung Kim Grant—was survived by two sons. One of her sons, Randy, says, "She died working for us." Perception, colored by fantasy, can mean protection or death sentence. For me—cis, white—it nearly always means protection. For others who have worked in erotic or even non-erotic massage, fantasies and perceptions about who are they are—what they might offer, where they might be from, how they might feel, what their working conditions might be—precipitate, time and again, brutal violence.

I attended a vigil for Yang Song in Flushing, weeks after she died. Her mother and her brother, Yumei Shi and Hai Song, were there, having come from China following her death, "hop[ing] to know the truth. We want to know whether this was a retaliation from the police and they forced her to die." Hai Song described his sister to *The Appeal* in opposition to the criminalizing fantasy the NYPD perpetuated around her, a fantasy they used to defend and excuse her death. Song said, "My sister indeed was a kind girl. She was not like what people might think she was. She even sent back milk formula from the U.S. for my son. And chocolates, presents as well. She often called my parents to talk to them even when she was busy because she knew this would make them happy."

Song was just working. She needed to make a living. Any fantasy beyond this was simply that, but the state sees what it wants to see—a fairy tale in which the death of a woman doing her job is justified: the raid, necessary; the parlor, a blight; the cops, good; the worker, at best, a casualty of their valiant cause.

In 2003, the performance artist Andrea Fraser made *Untitled*, a sixty-minute video recording of herself having sex with an unidentified art dealer at the Royalton Hotel in New York. To participate in the artwork and buy a copy of the film, the dealer paid an amount that was incorrectly reported, at the time, to be around $20,000. Fraser never disclosed the actual sum; to her, the symbolic importance lay in the fact of the transaction, not its amount. Nonetheless, the rumored price became an obsession. She told *T: The New York Times Style Magazine*, in 2019, "So that's what was the most painful for me, being exposed publicly in the art economy as cheap." Cheap for the art world, it's true, but wildly expensive for prostitution. A 2004 review of the piece in the *New York Times Magazine* begins by quoting Fraser: "'My first thought was, If I'm going to have to sell it, I might as well sell it,' [she] said last week . . . Fraser was referring in a starkly literal sense to her work's medium: a fit 38-year-old brunette in a sexy red V-necked dress, who is in fact herself." Here, Fraser states the reason a lot of people prefer sex work to other forms of service work—waitressing and bartending chief among them—done in order to support the work they actually want to produce. If you're selling some semblance of sex anyway, smiling and flirting for tips, you might as well sell the real thing for more.

In her interviews, though, Fraser was careful to distance the piece from run-of-the-mill sex work, and rightfully so. To the *Brooklyn Rail*, she explained,

> "Untitled" is about the art world, it's about the relations between artists and collectors, it's about what it means to be an artist and sell your work—sell what may be, what should be, a very intimate part of yourself, your desire, your fantasies, and to allow others to use you as a screen for their fantasies. It's not really about sex work, it's not really about prostitution, and it's not about getting my fifteen minutes.

While "allow[ing] others to use you as a screen for their fantasies" is a quite apt description of prostitution, what transpires in her piece isn't, really. What Fraser makes is a platonic ideal version of both sex work and the kind of erotic quid-pro-quo encounter that happens frequently in the art world: the price is high; the terms are clear; the subsequent solo show, guaranteed.

At the time, though, not everyone bought into Fraser's distinction between her piece and *real* prostitution. The Pulitzer Prize–winning critic Jerry Saltz began a 2007 *Artnet* article on Fraser's later work with a quote from an unnamed fellow critic: "Andrea Fraser is a whore." Though Saltz claims he defended her from the accusation, his own review of

Untitled, published in the same publication three years earlier, is more equivocal; he gives credit to the bravery of this particular performance, but says he's "never been a big fan of Fraser or her brand of institutional critique art . . . Above the shoulders Fraser is this nerdy looking girl with glasses and a pinched face; below the shoulders she's this worked-out Super Theory Woman." I suppose he means she has a big brain and a hot body, but he doesn't particularly like what she does with either. Saltz describes the sex itself as "stilted and rote and detached and strained (although I must say it looks as if she gives an attentive blow job). She's in excellent shape for a 39 year old." Incidentally, his commentary convinced me of *Untitled*'s likeness to what I know to be *actual*—standard—sex work, though I couldn't judge for myself, because I've never seen the film, only stills. Though the job is to convince the client that the sex we are having is precisely not rote or detached or strained—that I am, in fact, loving it—we all have our moments where we just can't fake it anymore. Giving head, of all things, is the easiest sex act to pretend to enjoy. A falsely enthusiastic blow job is a breeze; a cock in my mouth could be anything—a popsicle, a paintbrush, a pen—and the rest of my body is free.

It's likely, though, that Fraser also distinguished her work from prostitution for legal reasons, not just conceptual ones. The *Times* review goes on,

> Article 230 of the New York State penal code refers, quite straightforwardly, to the sort of exchange "Untitled" immortalizes as prostitution. It is safe to assume that transactions just like it are taking place this very minute in hotel rooms around the world. But those enterprises, unlike Fraser's, lack the frisson of what the art press tends reflexively to call "transgressive."

Through the lens of the law, Fraser's piece is a multifaceted crime, with a number of actors implicated. Friedrich Petzel Gallery set up the financial exchange on her behalf, which is, technically, sex trafficking. As a workaround, she might argue that what transpired was pornography, not prostitution—the former still existing in a legal gray area in New York, but less overtly criminalized than the latter. But in the end, what makes Fraser's work art, and not crime, is only that she calls it art, that she has a pre-existing, monied audience who will treat it as such, and that she has enough institutional clout to make her an unappealing legal target. I'm not criticizing; the same is true for me.

I've worked in the Royalton myself—the very same Royalton as Fraser—for a lower rate, but having a similar experience. The first time, I was meeting a client whom I was seeing for the second time. I'd met him a month prior, at a hotel further downtown, and he bit my inverted nipples so hard they appeared briefly extroverted, though they were only swollen. This client told me repeatedly he had a crush on me, a child-like word for a middle-aged man to use. He asked what kind of drink I'd like for our second meeting, and I chose whiskey. When I met him in the Royalton room, he presented me with a tiny bottle of Johnny Walker Black Label scotch and a tumbler holding one large ice cube, already melting. The room felt like an oversized submarine, or a luxury cabin below deck on a cruise ship, something about the sunken-in bed and the circular windows. We drank on the couch—the couch I imagine Fraser sitting on with her patron, flush with the knowledge of the sale, and the ensuing act that would execute it—and my client spanked me, which I prolonged. If I'm getting paid, attempts at pain are more palatable than attempts at pleasure. I think a lot of working girls feel the same.

I enjoy turning myself into an object for a man. Or rather, of all the strange ways to use my body, it's one I'm drawn to most reliably. Berlant opens *Cruel Optimism* with a definition for the common phrase "object of desire": "We are really talking about a cluster of promises we want someone or something to make to us and make possible for us. This cluster of promises could be embedded in a person, a thing, an institution, a text, a norm, a bunch of cells, smells, a good idea." And they go on, "To phrase 'the object of desire' as a cluster of promises is to allow us to encounter what's incoherent or enigmatic in our attachments, not as confirmation of our irrationality but as an explanation for our sense of our endurance in the object, insofar as proximity to the object means proximity to the cluster of things that the object promises."

Sometimes when I'm paid, I get high on my client's sense of his own endurance, which in that moment is accessed only through me. I'm evidently a portal—not in the sense of a trite, vaginal metaphor—but in the sense of a body facilitating nearness to youth and beauty, vigor, tenderness, the past, the future. Leonard Cohen writes,

> I go on and on
> about a noble young woman
> who unfastened her jeans
> in the front seat of my jeep
> and let me touch
> the source of life
> because I was so far from it.

This was my favorite poem for a long time, until it fell out of my favor because of what I perceived as its biological essentialism. I've changed tunes now, though, reading the source of life not as a particular body part but as young lust, which for Cohen—like for so many clients, and indeed, like for so many people who want to fuck—exists at the moment of the vital girl, whether nineteen, twenty-six, or thirty-eight, pulling off her underwear just for him.

My client bit my nipples again, and I excused myself to the bathroom, shoving a haphazardly torn makeup sponge inside myself. I was at the end of my period and didn't want to get any blood on the white Royalton sheets. When I emerged, he grasped at me, citing his crush again, and I became visible to myself as he saw me. I was the cluster of promises. For him, it was the promise of capacity—and isn't the hopeful promise of capacity what a crush really is—his capacity to please me, and my capacity to be enchanted by his efforts, uninterrupted by our age difference, or our lack of knowing one another, or an inconvenient rush of blood. *If good art makes you feel something*, I thought, *then I might be the best you've ever had.*

I used to want to be making art with everything I did; I wanted it all to count. I know now that it doesn't. I just have to make money in some way, so that I can spend the rest of my time doing what I want to do. Sometimes that way is more interesting than others; sometimes it gives me material to write and think about, or at least idly laugh about, like haltingly pissing in a guy's mouth on Wall Street, trying and failing to achieve a steady stream. I fucked a client in his boss's sublet one early fall morning, and, confronted by streaming, perfect sunlight when I left, I felt a rush of delight at the absurd illicitness of it all. Usually, though, sex work is neither glamorous nor creative nor fulfilling; it's precarious, well-paid labor, as mundane as it is strange.

I'm not sure how to address the looming reality that sex is the center of my life, and thereby the center of my creative work. If it's a trap—and I'm quite sure it is—I'm not willing to fight it right now. Tiqqun writes, "Every Young-Girl is an automatic, standard converter of existence into market value." If for Young-Girls our existence is always already defined by sex, then we are, by definition, converting sex into market value. We do this literally, and we do this in our art. But I'd probably do well to heed Fraser's warning: "I've always wanted attention, although I would have preferred to get this kind of attention for some other things I've done."

On Violation

In 2010, about to turn eighteen, I went alone to MoMA to see *The Artist Is Present*, the retrospective of Marina Abramović's work. I stepped between two naked people on either side of a relatively narrow doorway, which felt more silly than provocative. The nudity was devoid of eroticism, unlike Abramović's on-site performance. Abramović sat in a chair in the museum's atrium, which she occupied seven hours a day for the duration of the show, over 700 hours, while museum-goers waited in line for their turn to sit across from her. I did not sit across from her. I did not want to wait in line.

Decades before this retrospective, in 1975, Abramović performed a piece called *Role Exchange* in Amsterdam. Having worked as an artist for ten years, Abramović decided to find a prostitute in the red light district who had worked as such for the equivalent duration, and to swap places with her on the night of her gallery opening. The prostitute attended the party at the gallery in Abramović's place while Abramović sat in the prostitute's window in the brothel district for three hours. Abramović described this piece in a 2009 interview: "She told me that she saw this as a business and that her body was completely divided emotionally from it . . . It was quite incredible to see how she could separate the emotional and the physical." At the opening itself, "they asked [the prostitute]: 'Do you like art? What do you know about art?' She said she didn't know anything about art but she knew 'all about fucking.'"

I put on a show in 2021 at a gallery in New York where I turned the space into an incall—a place where sex workers host clients. There was a bed, and a kind of sitting room, and self-portraits on the walls, and I offered visitors different kinds of available appointments to speak with me or otherwise solicit interactions. In the gallery, people asked me all kinds of invasive questions. Poor at setting boundaries, I usually answered. A heterosexual couple came; the woman was interested both in hiring a sex worker and in becoming a sex worker, though she assured her boyfriend, sitting across from me on the couch, that she "never actually would." Her boyfriend asked if I had kids. What he meant to say was, "How would you explain your work to your kids?" Rather than telling him to fuck off, I answered sincerely, and only afterward registered the indignity of his question. "I guess I would tell them, Mommy's an artist," I offered, signifying my belief that identifying as an artist gives one license to do as they please without fear of judgment or condemnation.

The man who asked me this was an addict in recovery, so he also asked why I had harm reduction materials for safer drug use out in the gallery, like fentanyl test strips and naloxone. I explained that I think all art spaces should have such materials on display and available to the public for free, as drugs line the fabric of the art world and overdose occurs with greater frequency, it seems, every day. Also, I told him, sex workers often do drugs with their clients, or at the very least are often in the company of clients doing drugs.

I don't think this happens with any greater frequency than it does in the general population. People tend to hire sex workers on their leisure time, and since many people take drugs recreationally, it's not uncommon to want to deepen one's reverie once a step toward the illicit has already been taken. Taking pains to avoid overdose is particularly important in the context of transactional sex; criminal activity is already taking place, ratcheting up potential charges, and the sex worker tends to fall in the position of blame, whether for possession, distribution, or accidental manslaughter. The sex worker, too, is at greater risk of overdose without life-saving intervention, as a client likely won't want to call for help should the person they've hired experience a medical emergency while using an illegal substance; such an event might ruin their reputation, or career, or marriage.

In her position in the red light district, Abramović was not patronized by any clients. Two potential clients came by; one, she explained, wanted to see the woman he was used to seeing and left upon learning she was absent, while the other "was really drunk and wanted to know the price, and it was too high for him. I could not lower the price—that was basically the only rule I had to respect. So he left." Of the impact performing her piece had on her perception of prostitution, she says,

> I see it now as from their point of view, as a real job, a job of selling the body without emotional attachment. But what happens in the process is that human emotions get fucked up . . . a lot of problems come up in the end with this work, like drug use . . . which is much the same thing that happens with artists. Many artists these days die from an overdose, because of the intensity of being an artist and the demand of society on them is so high . . . both prostitutes and artists often come to the same end.

Abramović appears fixated on the idea of using the body "without emotional attachment," that the body and mind might be cleanly severed. I can attest to this: it's not so much that what happens is not felt in the moment but that almost immediately following it slides off the body like water from feathers. I once spoke of this phenomenon to a curator, who asked if I enjoyed sex in the context of work. Because I was attracted to him and enjoyed speaking with him, the question didn't bother me as much as it might have, and I said enjoyment was irrelevant. In a work context, one self-effaces. He suggested such disappearance from the self was an effort to disconnect, to escape the event, and I said, "Sure, of course, but certainly not more so than one escapes the self in any other workplace."

Some people need drugs to do this; some might prefer drugs to do this but work sober just as often. A glass of wine or a well-timed martini has often been integral to making the time pass easily for me, though I'm careful with my level of intoxication when spending time with someone paying for access to my body. I have friends who take Oxy, or Xanax, or Adderall, or Ambien, or methamphetamine—before working at a hotel with a client, or before working at a studio on a piece of art or writing.

Nan Goldin's extraordinary slideshow *The Ballad of Sexual Dependency*, first exhibited in the early 1980s and published as a book in 1986, documents herself, her friends, and her loved ones—many of whom were drug users, sex workers, artists, and drag queens—throughout the 1970s and '80s. Goldin became addicted to OxyContin in 2014, after doctors prescribed the drug for a surgery recovery. "It was the cleanest drug I'd ever met," she writes, "When I ran out of money for Oxy I copped dope. I ended up snorting fentanyl and I overdosed." Of the prostitutes that came into the Times Square bar she worked at for half a decade in the 1980s—the period in which she was taking photos for *Ballad*—Goldin says, "prostitutes drank Long Island iced tea; they wanted to get as drunk as possible on one drink." I believe it.

The poet Rachel Rabbit White writes of her years as a sex worker,

never thought of a dick in my mouth
as anything
but an interval
my pussy as nothing
but a vortex
and if I've suffered
I surely never felt it.

Going elsewhere is part and parcel of sex work. Attempting to abandon one's mind while a particularly unpleasant sensation is taking place in one's body happens often: an aggressive tongue in an ear; a tender caress of hair, repulsive in its attempt at true intimacy; a condom drying out after entering and exiting too many times, ripping at the seams of the body. Dissociation simultaneously flags and glosses over violation, two states that are part and parcel of capitalism.

Several summers ago, I worked in an office. I worked for a publishing company, a glorified assistant in all aspects ranging from PR efforts to mailing packages. It was easy. For a so-called 9 to 5 job, the actual hours were merciful (10 to 6); the office flexible and frequently all but empty. Nevertheless, I hated it. I did not like having to be at the same place every day, having at least thirty-five hours of my week taken from me for tedious tasks I had no feeling for. Once, sitting through a staff meeting, I thought I might scream. The skin-crawling feeling was the same as in bad moments of sex work: as though if I didn't exit the situation I might choke, or die, or bite someone. The intolerance becomes physical; I flex my calf muscles, grind my teeth. I finally excused myself from the meeting, rushed to the park outside and burst into tears, calling my boyfriend. "I can't do this," I said. "I can't do this work." This is to say: it's work that is intolerable; the oppressive fact of wage labor that drives us to dissociate, to exit our bodies or else inhabit them in the worst of ways, like a smoke-blind person attempting to crawl their way out of a fire, desperately trying to evade the source of the damning heat.

Of course, I can do wage labor, and I have, and I do. I have held many jobs; many are fine. But fine is not how life should be. I firmly believe that no one should have to work to live, that the imperative to sell one's labor in exchange for the fulfillment of basic survival needs is a foundational violation. Of retiring from sex work, Charlotte Shane writes, "I want this chapter of my life to be over. But if 'this chapter' is understood to be earning income through any labor as opposed to specifically earning income through sex, I will have to wait many years for it to end." Some portions of this chapter have been more offensive than others. I worked as a hostess at a popular brunch restaurant for the better part of a year; I spent mornings explaining to entitled parents that their family of four would have to wait two hours to sit. Enraged, their spittle reaching across my hostess stand, they would gesticulate wildly toward the empty tables in front of us. No matter how many times I explained that a system was in place—that other waiting families had been texted from my iPad and were on their way back to claim these tables within eight minutes—the parents grew redder in the face, speaking to me as though I were both stupid and vindictive. During the same period, a client spat on me and a colleague, getting his spittle on my chest and in my hair, and slapped us. You can imagine in which case my hourly rate was higher; you can imagine in which case I felt more violated.

There is a human appetite for violation, which many artists have made the subject of their work. In *Rhythm 0*, performed in 1974, Abramović stood for six hours alongside a table, upon which sat myriad objects and the following written instructions:

There are 72 objects on the table that one can use on me as desired.

Performance.

I am the object.

During this period I take full responsibility.

Duration: 6 hours (8pm – 2am)

One of the objects was a loaded gun. She says, "I felt really violated: they cut up my clothes, stuck rose thorns in my stomach, one person aimed the gun at my head, and another took it away. It created an aggressive atmosphere." Yoko Ono, too, invited a violation of sorts in *Cut Piece* (1964), wherein she invited audience members to cut off pieces of her clothing with scissors and keep the piece they cut. In 2016, Abel Azcona performed *La Guerra*, presenting himself, sedated with narcotics, to an audience whom he allowed to use his body without constraint.

I have made art about violation, too, and what it has helped me understand is less the unique impact of any particular violation on the body, but the pervasiveness of violation itself through all spheres of labor and social life under capitalism. My body often feels strained after I work, having been contorted in an unnatural or uncomfortable way. But my body feels strained, too, after sitting at a desk; after writing, or scheduling tweets for a company, or picking up a crying child who refuses to walk a step further, as I did for years, babysitting. The body at work is necessarily traumatized, destroyed; this is more true in some jobs than in others. I do not find it to be particularly true in highly paid prostitution. I understand the impulse to submit to the whims of others, the curiosity at how far a person might go. But there is a difference between someone taking something from you, and a priori giving that thing away by virtue of absconding a limit. I do not wish anything to be taken from me. I wish to give freely, or to sell.

In *Desire/Love*, Lauren Berlant writes, "A psychoanalytic model that locates the truth of a person in sexuality has been central to many of the modern narratives and norms that organize personal and institutional life." I have been ensnared by this model. If sexuality were key to the truth of who I am, I would organize my life around it. And yet: I understand the feminist anti-sex-work position. Or rather, I can imagine myself, having gone down a slightly different intellectual path, landing there. I don't have empathy for those who haven't thought beyond it—who remain stuck in the most simplistic, always bio-essentialist urge to protect women, and who refuse to consider the material violence they are inflicting upon said women by making it harder for us to earn a living—but I understand what might lead one, out of fear, to loathe prostitution.

Charlotte Shane writes,

> Before I was a sex worker, I was a fresh feminist who didn't like sex work . . . In this mentality, sex work, specifically prostitution, is seen as the logical culmination of all other commodification/commercialization of female sexuality and physicality . . . The end point is men using women's bodies for their own sexual pleasure, violently or at least callously. Men consume, women are consumed . . . This is a terrifying state of affairs. It's such a convincing nightmare that merely summarizing it leaves me momentarily paralyzed. And I know that the same emotional reaction swims underneath most feminist contemplation of the sex industry . . . We are all acquainted with malicious men who revel in their privilege. Catching a whiff of one can deliver us into hopelessness.

Men do use my body for their own sexual pleasure—and they might do so callously—but to say it like that removes my agency from the scenario entirely. I, too, understand the feminist position arguing that my consenting to sex work within a framework of violent and patriarchal capitalism isn't real consent; that I don't have true agency to sell my body under conditions wherein it is always already sold and sexualized. But that belies my feeling.

It is not that participating in my own consumption doesn't have a disturbing quality; that I don't ever wake up with a start in the night, wondering about my commodification of my own self and its impact on my psyche. It is not untrue that I am devastated when, in the context of work, I encounter a malicious man—a person whose entire personal and sexual gratification seems to flow from speaking hatefully toward girls while negotiating the price of their bodies. My friend sent me a screenshot of a text from a client she was making plans with; her rate came up, and he scoffed, telling her modelesque twenty-two-year-olds were charging less across the board. When she said that was fine but she did not discount, he remarked that he had never *had* an artist, but it might be worth it for the novelty. I felt nauseous. I told her not to see him if she didn't have to; it is frightening to look someone in the face whose desire for you is mixed with fury and contempt for the conditions that have brought him to you, that have made him feel unable to have the experiences he wants with women without paying for them. He feels small, and stepped on, and thus wants you to feel small and stepped on, too. This is a terrifying and dangerous place to be.

I met a young man in an art world context. He wanted to know more about my work. I offered him something to drink; he had whiskey, and I had wine. I drank a bit, though I wasn't particularly drunk. He drank a lot, and seemed fine, so I didn't think much of it. We spoke, in fact, very little about my work; he spoke about his recent breakup, and his work in tech futurity, and his psychotic boss, and his new foray into medicating his depression. I felt distinctly that he wanted something from me and relaxed into the power of that knowledge. His desire was stronger than mine in our meeting, and I enjoyed being able to rest, forcing him to act if his desire overpowered him. I didn't care much what transpired between us, but I had the sense that I could mold it to my advantage—for money, or connections, or both—should I choose to.

He touched my leg and said something offhand about how he was, obviously, attracted to me. I just stared at him.

He leaned over to kiss me, and we kissed, and then he suggested we lie down, and I said we wouldn't be having sex. I said he couldn't afford it. "I can," he said brashly, "I have money." He asked what we could do, and I said that if he Venmo-ed me a thousand dollars then and there, I would give him a blow job. I was amusing myself more than anything. He Venmo-ed me, and then, seemingly for no reason, sent a second payment, more than the first. I realized, with a start, how fucked up he was.

I asked if he was okay, and he waved away my concern and pulled his pants down. He couldn't perform, so to speak, and I became increasingly concerned about his level of intoxication. I felt strange and mildly panicked, having never been in a sexual situation with someone who was drunk enough that I was concerned about their ability to consent. Since money was involved, it felt like extortion.

I called a cab for him on his phone, walked him to it, and put myself in one, too. As he got in, he asked if I was coming with him; I told him no, and he appeared wistful, confused. The next morning I texted him, "How are you feeling?" He said he was sweating out the whiskey and that the events of the previous night were hazy. He apologized for drinking so much: "I was nervous, and I think my new meds affect my alcohol tolerance in a way I don't quite have a handle on yet." He asked if I would write him a play-by-play of what had transpired. We were writing back and forth on iMessage; I composed a long paragraph, explaining the chain of events as I recalled them—the kiss; the financial agreement; the multiple payments; the brief head; the cabs—and, as I was about to send it, his typing bubble reappeared. I had taken a while to respond because I was remembering and writing, but, evidently, he thought my pause indicated reticence to say something—he wrote, "Of course, no worries if you don't want to write all of that on this platform." I rolled my eyes at my carelessness. "I'm so dumb," I wrote back. "I was about to send a whole message, let's move to Signal."

After I explained, he admitted he was confused by the dual payment. Overcome with anxiety, I offered to send all the money back; after all, I'd done little work. It was interesting to be in what I tend to think of as a gendered situation but with the roles reversed—which is to say, I was suddenly concerned about getting MeToo-ed, something I'd only ever considered as someone on the victim end before. I was disoriented by my inability to discern if I'd been coercive: Would he have paid me money for sex if he was sober, and entirely in control of his faculties? Yet I was relatively certain that he had gotten so drunk precisely to work up the liquid courage to solicit me. He said he felt fine about the first payment but, if I wouldn't mind, would appreciate my return of the second. I hadn't cashed out my Venmo yet, so I simply sent the money back and watched the available balance halve.

We saw one another again. I told him over text that we could have a transactional sexual relationship, or simply be friends, and he said we should try the latter. I knew that wasn't what he really wanted, though, and when we met again, we did have sex, and he didn't pay for it. This time, I was drunk—two and a half martinis in—but more so, I sought a different type of trade. He offered his media connections; I fucked him.

Weeks went by, and what he'd promised me proved slow to pan out. We messaged occasionally on Instagram. My desire to see him—strong at first, fueled by the intrigue of new sex and the newness of bartering—waned. More weeks went by.

On a Saturday at midnight, he texted, "I want to hang out let's make a plan," failing to use any punctuation. I was viscerally put off. It read as presumptuous, the first clause beginning "I want," the second assuming my acquiescence.

I had enjoyed spending time with the kind of guy I used to hang out with for free—the kind of guy that, in another context, years earlier, I would have not only dated in my personal life but also pined for, excused all sorts of childish behavior for, and accommodated at midnight on a Saturday—for a clear exchange of payment or trade. I had felt older and wiser setting up a barter, but now I felt silly—legible exchange to me had clearly become mere casual sex for him. Countless men have told me, exasperated, "Not everyone thinks about this stuff as much as you." I did not respond. The next day he followed up: "Like maybe lunch this week?"

Charlotte Shane writes, "I know it's one type of power to 'take' someone's money. But it's a better type of power to not want anything they could give you." At a certain point, I no longer wanted to want anything this guy could give me, and at another later point, I simply no longer wanted it. It stopped feeling like a type of power to "take" from him. The taking had become work, unpaid at that—first the bartered sex, and then the work to recoup what he had promised me.

As I continued to ignore him, though, he continued to try and reach me. Suddenly, he wanted to make what he had promised me would happen, happen. I had ceased caring whether it did or didn't; many other more interesting things had transpired in between the promise and the failure to keep it. But I was curious about what made him feel—or rather, realize—that he owed me. And this owing opened up a whole new kind of power, one I felt frightened of, at first, and then excited by. I wondered if his move toward fulfilling his end of the deal was motivated by his own kind of gendered, consent-based fear of having violated our agreement. I wondered if I felt badly, at all, if it was.

He moved to make the introductions and connections he'd initially promised, and I went through with the meetings, because I figured, why not? He subsequently said that he wanted to interview me for a publication, and I agreed. I knew I didn't want to fuck again, so I offered a relatively brief window of time on a Friday—early evening—or else a phone call. He took me up on the early evening offer, suggesting a restaurant in the Meatpacking District for drinks. He got to the restaurant first. I arrived, and we sat down, and almost immediately he said something that pawned off the expressed purpose of this meeting—an interview—onto another, suggesting a future meeting a few weeks on. He implied that we didn't have time for an interview at the present moment, that we should just catch up. I was flooded with disdain.

In spite of knowing I should, I didn't leave. I stayed, ordering a cheese plate, and I listened to him tell me about his new relationship, which he had entered into since the last time he saw me. He was happy, he said. He wanted to marry her, he said. She knew all about me, he said, and, at this, I was patently bewildered: we weren't meant to mean something to one another, such that either of us would take up enough space to be presented, albeit historically, to a new partner. I said I was happy for him, over and over, because I didn't know what else to say. I wasn't not happy for him, but I just didn't care, and I loathed being ensnared into friendly drinks under false pretenses and being asked to soothe his ego, to congratulate him on being no longer romantically down and out, but secure and desired. Psychic manipulation upsets me as much as or more than physical manipulation, because it treads on my belief that I can outsmart anyone playing at such a game. Affronts to my intellect are always more lasting, personally, than affronts to my body.

In the end, we each violated the other. I proceeded with sex and money without realizing he was too drunk; he delayed and breached the terms of our agreement; I've written about him here, without his permission, in an unkind way.

In her book *Porn Work: Sex, Labor, and Late Capitalism*, Heather Berg asks, "How should we talk about consent when there is rent to pay?" Such a question is relevant both in the context of sex work and in the context of workplace sexual harassment. Such a question also illuminates the failures of MeToo as it was mainstreamed: the failure to meaningfully address this question and to allow for all the gray areas of coercion and exploitation that would have to be part of any honest answer. When not couched in an explicitly anti-capitalist analysis, reformist movements to improve conditions for women facing misogyny and sexual violence at work implicitly value the testimonies of some women over others—those in respectable jobs; those operating within formal workplaces—and fail to address the foundational structures of workplace abuse, sexual and otherwise, endemic to late capitalism. Absent an anti-work politic, the movement left out large swaths of women participating in underground and illegal economies, while championing the ascension of women in the ranks of abusive institutions and corporations built on the backs of un- and under-paid gendered, racialized, and coerced labor.

In July 2020, an anonymous Instagram account appeared under the handle @cancelartgalleries. The account posts stories followers send in about workplace abuses, exploitations, and microaggressions suffered at art galleries in New York City. In an opinion piece for *Hyperallergic*, the person or group behind the handle writes, "As discrimination and exploitation becomes buried under meaningless words like 'diversity,' the evil that is the generational wealth of white people remains intact. The hundreds of submissions to our anonymous form have made clear that the art world's concessions made for representation politics have failed."

In February 2021, a former summer intern submitted a post recounting their experience at Gagosian, one of the most influential galleries worldwide: "I felt so grateful and lucky to be chosen after a really rigorous interview process. I had no idea I would spend the entire summer with the accounting and finance department . . . shredding Larry Gagosian's private records and expense reports detailing his partying, client gifts (which included 'dinners' with expensive 'entertainment'), lingerie for female staff (when is that appropriate please?) . . . I think I spent that entire summer in flat out shock." This is a lot of things, but it's not shocking. The thing is, it's really not wrong for a wealthy man to gift a whore to a client. This is the kind of thinking that would get me excommunicated by most feminists, but: if she's paid well, it's perfectly fine. It's wrong to buy lingerie for female staff, though I'd bet that lingerie was actually for the "entertainment." Maybe that's me being naive, though. An artist commented, "Sorry but I don't want to show with a gallery that DOESNT expense lingerie and drugs. Who cares? This is just another day in nyc." In this economy, I don't entirely disagree.

I am endlessly curious about who the wealthiest of the wealthy in New York's art world are hiring for sex, though I dare not name any names for fear of a libel suit at even the suggestion. I know so many expensive girls. And yet. The answer might be that they are hiring no one—there are people who wield enough power and influence that they do not have to hire anyone. In a workplace, they might delude themselves that any erotic game between them and their underlings is, in fact, not just consensual but also desired, because they are not paying, additionally, for it, and because people want so many things from them other than money. And off the clock, more beautiful young people who want things from them emerge, eager to date or fuck or have affairs in the hope of securing a job, a sale, an introduction, or a show—or simply to feel proximate to the shiny glinting objects, money, and power. Another post about Gagosian reads, "One summer Larry came to visit a newly opened show at his London gallery . . . One of the unpaid and very overqualified interns didn't quite look 'the part' (comments were made about her size and scruffy look) and she was asked to wait in the stationery/printing cupboard during his visit. She had to wait there for over an hour!" The difference between the whores hired by dealers, collectors, mega-artists, and cultural tastemakers and the gallery girls, assistants, and unpaid interns at their beck and call is that the former are paid to be sexualized, objectified, and sometimes degraded, while the latter are not even paid adequate wages for what's in their job description, let alone harassment tacked on. The refusal to acknowledge sexual labor as such, alongside the conspiratorial dickriding between those on top who need to sell and those on top who might buy, simultaneously produces and relies upon webs of quotidian violences at the expense of pools of workers rendered disposable, replaceable, and *lucky* for the opportunity.

When he was formally accused of a decade of sexual harassment in a lawsuit against his magazine, Knight Landesman, lionized publisher of *Artforum*, resigned in 2017. Plaintiff Amanda Schmitt sought $500,000 in damages. In an initial statement on the lawsuit, *Artforum* attempted to deny Schmitt's legitimacy, stating that when she contacted the magazine about the harassment she was experiencing in 2016, the magazine "took companywide steps to address any workplace transgressions." The statement went on: "Her subsequent claim for damages, in 2017, one year after her initial complaint, appears to be unfounded, and seems to be an attempt to exploit a relationship that she herself worked hard to create and maintain." In response, more than 2,000 signatories—including gallerists, artists, curators, and art world administrators, self-defined "workers of the art world"—published an open letter in the *Guardian*, asserting:

> We are not surprised when curators offer exhibitions or support in exchange for sexual favours. We are not surprised when gallerists romanticise, minimise, and hide sexually abusive behaviour by artists they represent. We are not surprised when a meeting with a collector or a potential patron becomes a sexual proposition. We are not surprised when we are retaliated against for not complying. Abuse of power comes as no surprise.

In 2021, Schmitt and *Artforum* settled for an undisclosed amount. Though *Artforum*'s initial statement had claimed that "at no time was Artforum complicit or culpable," an internal email produced as a result of legal discovery demonstrated the pervasiveness of Landesman's "transgressions" and the futility of attempts to stop his serial harassment such that the workplace environment might indeed be considered complicit. In a 2017 email from one co-publisher, Charles Guarino, to another, Tony Korner, Guarino recalled, "I remember . . . two years ago . . . telling Knight (knowing nothing of Amanda at the time) that his behavior toward women had to stop, to change. It could really hurt all of us, I asserted. He became angry, clenched his fists. 'I'm never going to stop. Never,' he said." No surprise, indeed.

There's a scene in the television series *Girls* that conveys a particular kind of hysterically needy and porous white femininity: a predilection for vulnerability stemming from a deeply held belief that nothing truly bad will ever actually happen to you, because the world is, in fact, structured for your protection; a predilection that then leads to a unique ability to court violation, if not safely, at least more safely than other women might have the privilege to do. I've remembered the scene for years, though I've forgotten nearly everything else that took place in the series. Hannah, the protagonist played by Lena Dunham, finds herself at a handsome divorced stranger's beautiful apartment, the result of a meet-cute at a coffee shop. Hannah is twenty-four, the guy forty-two, and when he invites her inside, she says out loud that she shouldn't, that she doesn't know him, and that he might be a serial killer, before promptly rushing through the door. After they have sex, she cries and reflects on her need "to take in experiences, all of them":

> There's all these experiences that I just feel like I've asked for, things where it's like, who in their right mind would want that? Like one time, I asked someone to punch me in the chest and then come on that spot. Like that was my idea, that came from my brain. And it's like, what makes me think I deserve that?

I relate to this desire to find violation, particularly of a sexual nature, interesting. I remember watching this episode in college, before I'd ever done sex work, and reflecting on things I'd said *yes* to primarily because of the same *why not*? I think I preferred the idea of truly asking for it, as opposed to the more frightening version, wherein I hadn't but someone acted as if I had. You hear the statistics, and you talk to your friends, and sometimes it seems like everybody you know, and everybody you ever might know, has been sexually assaulted or raped. And if this was the case, I reasoned, maybe it was better to get out ahead of it and say yes to everything, if everything was going to happen to me anyway. That way, I could study it; I could master it; I could find it curious and informative, as opposed to jarring or disturbing.

I met a client about two years ago whom I was attracted to. He was older and, about to sell a company, was poised to become even wealthier than he already was, which was unrestrainedly so. He told me he was extremely smart, and that he had never been in love. He was the classic romantic archetype for me: a standoffish, narcissistic man who professed to feel nothing but whose heart I felt sure I could melt. A chance for me to assert dominance through desirability, the only way I like to be dominant.

The hotel we met in was full of subliminal messages about capitalism's largesse: every room I've been in there has housed either Walter Isaacson's biography of Steve Jobs or Ayn Rand's *Atlas Shrugged*. He told me tragedies that had happened in his life, and I pushed and probed, asking for more detail. He remarked that he was dangerously close to spending more of our time talking than fucking, but then he gestured toward the space between us and said, "That's part of what this whole thing is for, anyway." I told him about the book I was writing. Eliding its more memoiristic possibilities, I described it as about "art, sex, and capitalism, theoretically." He laughed, and then said he was an expert on all three subjects. Though he was just on the edge of insufferably pretentious, I developed a crush on him. I liked how he made no attempt to keep me for any length of time; he assured me I could leave whenever I wanted, more than once, and he was the only client I've ever had who earnestly seemed to mean it.

He told me that, when you are about to sell a company, and "money people" know you are about to sell a company, they swoop in, in the hopes of managing your new money. He was receiving calls from Goldman and all of the other top investment banks; everyone was telling him to buy art and warehouse it. He said that there was such a way he would be able to pay no taxes on the sale—offshore banks and the like—but that he wouldn't do that, though it was tempting. He believed in paying taxes; he thought the wealthy should be taxed even more. We met a second time the day after the Trump-Biden election; he said we should keep our meeting unless "the streets are on [fire emoji]," and I didn't tell him I hoped they would be. When he disparaged the rioting of the George Floyd rebellion the summer before, offering the typical liberal line that police reform would be welcome but abolition "ridiculous," I nodded along. I told him I was further left than he was, but kept my anarchism and reverence for property destruction to myself. We watched the pundits comment on the ambiguous results on television, and he predicted Biden's win.

He drank vodka on ice while I drank natural wine, and he unbuttoned my white dress and told me to sit on the bed. I explained myself as submissive, and while at first he said he didn't find himself to be dominant, he evidently was. He pulled his belt off and put it around my neck—loosely, but around my neck nonetheless. Choking is a hard limit for me at work; though I'll submit to someone whom I find non-threatening because it comes easiest to me, I'm not stupid. Or rather, I didn't think I was stupid, and then I let him put a belt around my neck, because I liked it, because death was all around us as fall turned to winter within a global pandemic, because I just wanted to see what it felt like, and because I did not believe that anything bad would happen to me. Nothing bad did, but I'm smart enough to recognize I was lucky, not right.

I only told one friend what I'd let him do afterward. "I think I like feeling like I'm about to die," I half whispered as we drove around our neighborhood in her car. In bed together, he'd said to me, "This is good, right?" His phrasing it as a question belied the uncertainty of someone who has paid another to be pleased. I didn't know how to answer other than, "I let you put your belt around my neck." I don't know if he understood the significance, but it seemed to satisfy him for the moment.

He stopped seeing me; I don't know why. He seemed like the kind of person who was loath to let himself be happy or attached. Perhaps he feared—or, less flattering, simply disliked—being around a person like me, who thought that what he wanted was to have his inner life pierced and examined. In reality, he probably wanted precisely the opposite, a simple escape. Sometimes I miscalculate another's desire for intensity.

I wrote to him to tell him of a show I was soon putting on, having already told him my first name and the subject of my book. I wrote to him through the online portal we had previously used, explaining that I'd lost his number, which wasn't technically true. He texted the next day, "I saw your note. I underestimated your fortitude and focus. I sensed the underlying abilities were present, but that often leads nowhere. Not to say I'm surprised, but rather oddly pleased and proud." It was so superior, so offensive.

"Will you commission me?" I asked. "I'm not sure," he answered, "but I'd love to see you again." He didn't commission me; he only texted me from time to time, gesturing at plans but never following through with them. When he would reach out to me, I felt alternately impatient, hopeful, and irritated.

About a year after we had last seen each other, he wrote on New Year's Eve day, "I was day dreaming about you yesterday. Remembering our natural connection/flow creates longing." The message was a bit saccharine, and he'd done nothing but waste my time making half-plans every other month, but still I responded. Again, for months, we batted our availability back and forth, until finally I was in residence in another gallery, charging $1,000 to enter the space. When he wrote to me that month, I invited him there. He accepted, saying he'd walk over that afternoon, and because of his tone and the immediacy of his responses, I believed him and felt satisfied in the way I do when I get exactly what I want: money and material for my work. A few hours passed, and he didn't show. I wrote, "Am I expecting you or am I leaving the gallery?" Five minutes later, he answered, "I'd rather see you like we did before. I don't want to be part of the art project." And only then did I feel a sense of violation, because I had let myself feel that he thought of me as an artist—that I was in control, finally, and not just calling the shots, but winning—when he never had any intention of participating in my work. But worst of all, I was humiliated that he used the word *project*, and not *work*—that in neither arena of my working life was my work seen as work, and that I was naive to imagine it could be viewed and understood as such.

The art and sex marketplaces are cynical and cruel, writ large. Both are intimately tied to state violence—through financially symbiotic entanglements between the state's disciplining apparatuses and the museum, or the adult ad site—and both are shaped by the whims of the powerful and hyper-wealthy, structured at every turn by racism, hyper-visibility, the policing of people and borders, and the bottom line of profit. Art institutions with shiny veneers platform diverse and progressive artists even as they are financially propped up by money from the sale of arms to state regimes committing profound human rights violations, covering up their complicity through public shows of good. Meanwhile, fantasies of the violations sex workers face in the sex industry, and the subsequent call to rescue them, lead the state to commit large-scale violations against workers, shutting down some companies workers rely on for ads and revenue while propping up others that cooperate with the government, ensnaring workers in a criminal-legal system that destroys lives and livelihoods alike.

In November 2017, the Department of Homeland Security raided the Eros Guide's call center in Youngsville, North Carolina. The operation was a search and seizure; agents spent the day and night poring over servers, documents, and computers. At the time, the US Attorney's Office confirmed a sealed, active investigation ongoing against Bolma Star Services, the Eros Guide's parent company, and a warrant was granted to investigate alleged "cross-border illegal activity," but they offered no further information on the nature of the case. To my knowledge, any details and resolution, or lack thereof, remain opaque.

The Eros Guide, a glorified adult classifieds platform, was founded in 2000 and quickly took over the lion's share of the escort advertising market through search engine optimization. I spoke to a friend once who referred to Eros's rise as "the gentrification of online advertising"; over time, as the most expensive and therefore lucrative site through which to post an ad, Eros became a signifier of status, one that girls had to adopt in order to reach a particular client base. On Eros, one can pay for additives like VIP Status, which offers little other than the option to animate and rotate one's thumbnail ad photo, and signifies to clients that the worker in question can afford to pay double for so little. The real point of VIP Status is not that clients care if your thumbnail is animated but that they can see you are successful and already top-earning, giving them the illusion that they're engaging the best, a worker who can afford to take on only clients she earnestly wants to see.

Advertising on Eros is technically legal; workers sell time, rather than sex. One cannot list acts or services one does and does not offer. Escorting falls squarely within the realm of Michel Foucault's "useful delinquency"—wherein "the existence of a legal prohibition creates around it a field of illegal practices, which one manages to supervise, while extracting from it an illicit profit through elements, themselves illegal, but rendered manipulable by their organization in delinquency." The law prohibits prostitution, putting escorting and its surrounding industries (advertising websites, web creators, SEO specialists, escort photographers) into legal gray areas, simultaneously sanctioned and not. Their position as useful delinquents makes workers in these industries even more precarious because the constant threat of shutdown gives companies greater power to abuse workers at will. Corporations like Eros, for example, have wild power to monopolize and extort those in need of their services because there are few other options and little legal recourse available to escorts when they are wronged. Eros frequently and somewhat randomly bans escorts for life, allowing some workers to show nudity on their profiles and dropping others for attempting to display less lewd photos. My friend who commented on Eros's gentrification of the industry was unceremoniously banned for attempting to post a new ad with a photo she'd used without incident countless times before; she had spent tens of thousands of dollars advertising over years through the site and obtained the majority of her new clients there.

My friend was kicked off after the raid, and after the passage of FOSTA/SESTA, which followed in April 2018. The House and Senate versions of the bill were, respectively, the Allow States and Victims to Fight Online Sex Trafficking Act and the Stop Enabling Sex Traffickers Act; the two were packaged together to roll back Article 230 protections that prevented websites from being held liable for hosted speech that might be construed as facilitating sex trafficking. At the time, Melissa Gira Grant reported,

> Sex workers and survivors of trafficking, as well as advocates for both communities, warned that the legislation and crackdowns on websites that could come in its wake would be dangerous for sex workers and survivors of trafficking alike. They argued that closing low-cost online ad sites like Backpage would drive sex workers out of indoor work spaces that allowed for discreet advertising and client screening and into the streets.

Indeed, this is exactly what happened. Backpage shuttered before the passage of FOSTA/SESTA, but many free or low-cost ad sites followed in the wake of the legislation. Workers speculated on which site would go down next. Eros continued to make changes to its terms of service but remained online. It became impossible to reach their customer service representatives, and lag times for submitted ads to pass internal review and appear online went from forty-eight hours to weeks. Touring workers completed their tours with their ads for cities they visited still sitting in purgatory, eventually posted well after they'd returned to their home base, useless. Photos and copy were rejected with no rhyme or reason;

attempting to pass through Eros's increasingly veiled review process became a routine of acrobatics and guesswork. Workers paid for ads in cryptocurrency to avoid their bank accounts being flagged or even shut down for affiliation with an adult site; when workers were banned from the platform, many had money sitting in their Eros accounts, prepaid in Bitcoin for future ads. Eros, however, reserved the right to terminate service without refund.

Of Eros's raid, Caty Simon, co-editor of *Tits and Sass*, writes,

> Over the past few years, Eros has required progressively more revealing ID checks in order to confirm advertisers are of age. Now those IDs, including those of migrant and undocumented sex workers, are in the hands of the Department of Homeland Security. Sure, if they use this evidence at all, the feds will probably just focus on those of us they can construe as traffickers—sex workers who own incalls for the use of other sex workers, for example. There's probably no reason for most Eros users to panic about this. Still, having your real name, address, and ID number in the hands of DHS is a nightmare scenario in a profession where our survival depends on our anonymity.

Since the raid, every few months, a story will make the rounds on Twitter that a worker was stopped at the border and questioned by agents of the Transportation Security Administration, an arm of DHS. These workers report that agents use their Eros ads as evidence of their illegal activity, questioning them about their engagement with trafficking and prostitution.

This is all hearsay, but it isn't difficult to imagine it to be true. The policing of prostitution is intimately tied to the policing of borders; the two emerged in modern life concurrently, fueled by rampant xenophobia and racist moralizing. Lorelei Lee writes,

> The first law limiting immigration into the United States, the Page Act of 1875 [prohibited] the "importation into the United States of women for the purposes of prostitution." The Page Act also prohibited the entering into a contract by immigrants from China, Japan, or "any Oriental country" for "lewd and immoral purposes." The law resulted in the exclusion of almost all Chinese women from the US, a move that the historian Jean Pfaelzer has described as ethnic cleansing.

From its inception, US efforts to restrict free movement through borders have weaponized the public's distaste for sex work. Today, the policing of borders continues to work toward ethnic cleansing.

In November 2018, a year after Eros's DHS raid, *Hyperallergic* published a report on the Whitney Museum board's vice chairman, Warren Kanders, and his ownership of the company Safariland, which produces tear gas used to terrorize migrants attempting to cross US borders. On November 25, 2018, agents of US Customs and Border Protection—DHS's largest federal law enforcement agency—attacked Central American migrants attempting to cross San Diego's border from Mexico, seeking asylum. The peaceful march of migrants included children, and photos were widely shared of the attack showing kids in diapers running from tear gas steadily releasing into the air. Reporters on the scene posted photos, as well, of the emptied tear gas canisters, branded Safariland.

Responding to *Hyperallergic*'s revelations, nearly one hundred Whitney staffers signed an open letter to museum leadership, demanding they "convey our concerns to the

Board, including that they consider asking for Warren Kanders's resignation." Meanwhile, Decolonize This Place, an "action-oriented movement and decolonial formation in New York City and beyond," began to stage actions at the Whitney, also calling for Kanders's resignation. Kanders responded to the staffers' letter, defending himself and his ownership: "While my company and the museum have distinct missions, both are important contributors to our society. This is why I believe that the politicization of every aspect of public life, including commercial organizations and cultural institutions, is not productive or healthy." Safariland tear gas was also used against protestors in Ferguson and Standing Rock; the company's slogan is *Together, We Save Lives*.

The controversy surrounding the Whitney's refusal to oust Kanders reached a fever pitch at the 2019 Whitney Biennial, showing a majority of artists of color and running from May through September. Decolonize This Place held weekly protests, while Verso published an open letter signed by hundreds of artists and writers asking the Whitney to remove Kanders. In July, artist and writer Hannah Black, and the writers Ciarán Finlayson and Tobi Haslett, published an open letter in *Artforum* titled "The Tear Gas Biennial," calling on biennial artists to remove their work from the show, expressing disappointment that to date there had been no meaningful refusal by participating artists and no boycott, and interrogating what, exactly, had "made refusal seem inappropriate or impossible." They refute both the argument that precarious artists being shown in the biennial cannot afford to remove their work—"as if [strike and boycott] were marks of luxury, rather than acts of struggle"—and the argument that demanding they boycott places "an unfair burden on artists of color," explaining that "this view promotes the reactionary fiction that marginalized or working-class people are the passive recipients of political activity as opposed to its main driver."

Arrestingly, the authors write:

> But we are concerned less with the state of the art world than with what this world does to our friends, peers, and elders, when professionalization at all costs becomes the condition of their practice. The ease with which left rhetoric flows from art is matched by a real poverty of conditions, in which artists seem convinced they lack power in relation to the institutions their labor sustains. Now the highest aspiration of avowedly radical work is its own display.

Commissioned to create a piece for the 2019 biennial, the London-based collective Forensic Architecture produced a short film utilizing new machine-learning technology to track the international use of Triple Chaser tear gas grenades, sold by Safariland for use against civilians. The sale and purchase of tear gas is not publicly available information; currently, the only method to track its economic movement is to gather visual evidence of its use on the ground. Forensic Architecture, in direct response to the conditions surrounding the biennial, used the opportunity to critique the practice of artwashing:

> What does Safariland gain through its sponsorship of and association with culture? Museums are many things. But most of all, they are a system of value exchange and symbolic capital. What is being traded in the Whitney Biennial is reputation. Our goal is to invert this economy. As participants in the biennial, the only response that felt responsible, and justifiable, was to turn the instruments of reputation-laundering, insofar as we had our hands on the controls, against those with the reputations to lose.

In July, Kanders resigned; the Whitney's director, Adam Weinberg, remarked, "Here's a man who has given a tremendous amount of his time and money to young, often edgy and radical artists . . . that's one of the ironies of all this." One hand should not wash the other, though; platforming some members of a marginalized group does not erase or make up for abuses against the rest.

Both Eros and the Whitney remain not only operational, but dominant in their respective industries. Both continue to platform people other institutions won't; that does not make either institution *good*. Both, as Forensic Architecture points out, traffic in reputation and monetize it. Each gets away with offering little or less than little in return to the workers who provide their content. The Whitney suffered another scandal in 2020 when public outcry forced the museum to cancel a show— "Collective Actions: Artist Interventions in a Time of Change," presented as a showcase of artist responses to Black Lives Matter uprisings and Covid—when numerous Black artists in the show were notified that the museum had acquired their work not through their galleries or studios, but from various fundraiser auctions, where the proceeds went to providing people financial relief from state violence and systemic failures. Such auctions were common throughout the uprisings and pandemic: artists donated work to be sold for greatly reduced prices, under the good-faith assumption that regular people, looking to support urgent causes, would purchase the pieces they'd received no remuneration for—not museums with healthy endowments finding snakelike ways to avoid paying market rate.

Little reportage exists on Eros, save for its mention in articles tracking prostitution-related arrests, but anecdotal evidence from friends suggests it's as useless and unavoidable as ever. I posted an ad in December 2021 and uploaded my passport to prove my legal age.

I did this in concert with a video I made, commissioned for a show curated by a person whose family's wealth touches many facets of the art world, wealth grown from arms dealing to an apartheid regime. I was asked to make a piece for a show loosely about art, sex, and technology, to be exhibited in part on the porn site Onlyfans; for a period, I struggled to decide whether to participate in the show. I wondered if I would allow myself to compromise my political allegiances to participate; I wondered if I would even benefit from participating, or if the stain of the family would ultimately stain me, losing me more opportunity than I would gain. Many artists whose work I respect have de-authored pieces in the family's permanent collection in protest of the occupation they support; many artists whose work I respect continue to work with the family, and an artist whose work I revere would be shown alongside mine. Though the starting point was violence on a global scale, my decisions revolved entirely around myself: the moral relativism I could live with; the impact on my reputation; the artwork I did and did not want to make.

Once I decided to participate, I struggled to decide whether to take the thousand-dollar honorarium that was offered to me. Ultimately, the piece I made was entirely and explicitly about the contours of these decisions, implicating myself, the family, and the larger structures that finance my life, all of us economic beneficiaries of border-based violence; I called the video *Dirty Calculations*. To date, this video—existing alongside the ad I posted in the city I traveled to, to celebrate the show's opening—remains one of my favorite pieces of art I've ever made. I also frequently regret making it, regret burning a bridge with a person and a family who might have otherwise continued to support my work, continued to provide access or opportunity. The work is good; it is also art, and it succeeds only at the level of art—it neither takes nor incites any politically meaningful action.

It's doubtful Eros is truly shadow-run by DHS, as workers speculate (perhaps why it was never shut down in the wake of FOSTA-SESTA), but it's reasonable to assume that DHS's many branches have access to Eros's files whenever they need to arrest, threaten, or otherwise limit free movement.

Meanwhile, the relationship between the art market and warfare remains potent as ever. The 2022 Venice Biennale opened two months after Russia's invasion of Ukraine; in late April, Venice saw an influx to its shores of artists, curators, oligarchs, and billionaires. *Artforum* contributor Kate Sutton reported,

> PinchukArtCentre announced that in lieu of its usual ritzy Future Generation Art Prize showcase, it would be putting on "This is Freedom: Defending Ukraine." . . . Instead of the traditional concert—Viktor Pinchuk has always known how to entertain—this year the opening featured a taped address from Ukrainian president Volodymyr Zelensky. (When I asked a friend why the embattled politician would possibly make time for this, he demurred, "Where else could you reach this many arms dealers under one roof?")

Artists and sex workers alike continue to organize against the oppressive conditions of their respective marketplaces, in some cases making significant strides. Nan Goldin's relentlessly dedicated group PAIN, formed to expose and fight the "toxic philanthropy of the billionaire Sackler family, who ignited the opioid overdose epidemic with their blockbuster drug, OxyContin," is an astonishing example. The Sacklers successfully laundered their reputation through massive funding of major museums; PAIN has since "through direct action . . .

successfully pushed many museums and universities to refuse Sackler funding and cut ties with the family," both remarkable victories. After the shutdown of Backpage and the passage of SESTA/FOSTA, a team of sex workers and technologists founded the ad site Tryst with the goal of offering free and low-cost advertising options to "sex workers of all genders and demographics," with membership "structured to be non exploitative and significantly less expensive than any other large verified platform." Nonetheless, it is hard not to feel all but hopeless when surveying the industries overall. The scope of fatalities on the hands of many who sit on boards, control interests, and direct raids, all while giving lip service to improved opportunities, conditions, and diversities, is breathtaking. But it remains easiest—if one wants to show and sell work; to access the most desired clients; to ascend the ranks in either industry, gaining status, success, and security—to simply appreciate the strategic bandages and finely wrought stitches, and ignore the copious blood flow underneath.

I handed in the first draft of this book and proceeded to work more in the immediate, subsequent months than I ever had in my life. I hadn't worked much while writing, and I wanted to start making bigger money again, and I knew to do that only by doing the thing I had been writing about.

I met a string of awful new people. I found myself in situations that I previously would have left, out of a slight sense of fear or a feeling that the person involved was wasting my time. But now, I was determined to get the money I was owed out of the situation. I was impressed by my own ability to grin and bear it, to guide the interaction toward a financial and physical end. I was also steadily drifting toward a rather all-encompassing disconnection from my self: a gossamer film seemed to cover me as I moved between domestic and working life, allowing less access to me for any individual client, but also allowing myself less access to my own personhood. It was strange. I looked in the mirror one day and I felt for the first time in a long time a palpable sense of dissociation, akin to a deep depression, though with less pain attached. I looked not far away but unreachable. My features were all there but didn't quite make sense.

I don't like writing about sex work this way—in any way that might give ammunition to the feminists who call for sex work prohibition—but it would be dishonest to pretend that dissociation isn't a consequence (or, more accurately and kindly, an enabler) of being in unpleasant sexual situations with strangers. I made a lot of money during this period. I don't regret the amount I worked.

I drove with my boyfriend to a wedding in his hometown, and I cried on the way back. I felt upset by something that had happened at work, and I hadn't spoken to him about it yet because I hadn't decided yet if I was truly upset, or just tired, and I also didn't want to upset him. In the car, for whatever reason, I decided I wanted to talk about it, and I described what happened.

I had agreed to see a client for a slightly lower rate than I normally would have, against my better judgment. He was a classic type, the kind of person who dangles seeing you a lot as a bargaining chip, explaining that he's not cheap, he just wants to find something sustainable. I only agreed when he suggested meeting at a very expensive hotel downtown, because I wanted to take marketing photos with a friend I was beginning to work with, and we figured we could use the room as a site for a shoot after he left.

Our plan was to meet in the lobby's bar. When we did, he explained that he lived right next door and that was where he wanted to spend our time together. This was a red flag; it's inappropriate to suggest a hotel as a meeting place and then bait and switch to your residence, as though the two are equally safe. However, it was the afternoon, and we were on a wildly monied block, with doormen and building staff abounding. I went upstairs with him, and he opened a bottle of red wine as I perused his apartment's meticulously designed but sterile decor—it was more like a personal hotel for someone who lives elsewhere but comes into the city on business with some frequency. We sat talking and I found his cheerful and kind demeanor pleasantly engaging. He was Irish, and, having grown up with an Irish babysitter and surrounded by Irish construction workers, I find that such an accent tends to put me at ease. He seemed sweet.

We moved to his bedroom, and he decided he wanted to make me squirt, something I can't do. He was aggressively finger-fucking me, and I was conscious of how much it hurt. I could have told him to do something else, but I reasoned that this was better than having his spit touch every part of me, or a particular kind of horrible tenderness. I thought, though, that his aggression was probably causing micro-lacerations, which would inevitably sting sharply when I tried to have sex in a way I liked, later on. I didn't really know what I wanted to do, so I lay there taking it for a bit, and then excused myself to the restroom, though I actually went to the living room, grabbing condoms and checking my phone. In spite of the finger-fucking, I felt fine. I stood briefly in his living room, sipping my wine and looking out at the park.

I walked back to the bedroom and I registered a few things: he had gotten his own condoms out, which were ribbed and lubricated in some absurd way—never a good sign for impending sex. I noticed a black chest-like object open across the room, filled with things that looked colorful, and then saw an enormous dildo on the bed. I'm not sure how to explain what I felt in that moment, other than a revulsion so pure that any fear of consequence left me. I spoke immediately, clearly: "You cannot fuck me with that." He tried to cajole me for a minute but I think sensed my level of seriousness and relented. I went into a rote mode, figuring the soonest and safest way to leave with my money would be to get him off, so I let him fuck me with his own cock. He was barely hard, and I remember thinking with dread that this would go on forever, until he moved me into a different position and within two short minutes it was over. I left.

I felt exhausted and foolish, but mostly blank when I left. As distance between myself and the encounter grew, though, the blankness hardened to hatred. What I had endured wasn't worth the money. I had been underpaid and made to look at an object intended to hurt me.

I had little other paid sex that month. But I had paid encounters that felt, in ways, worse. I met new clients under the guise that perhaps we were simply meeting for a drink, but if all went well, a previously agreed upon amount of money would change hands. I had dinner with a man who was visiting from California who seemed like a good, mildly eccentric person. He professed to have no issue with paying for my time, regardless, saying he simply wanted me to feel comfortable, and to only do anything else with him if I really wanted to. He felt it was "anti-feminist" to abhor the idea of paying for a woman's time. He was evolved. As I sat down for dinner, he handed me a card he'd picked out, knowing I was a writer, that had a drawing of a person at a desk surrounded by books on it. Inside the envelope were five hundred-dollar bills, splayed out; that was the amount he'd chosen for social compensation, and I figured it wasn't bad for an hour of relatively easy but tiresome chitchat. I told him I'd made my first film recently, and that it was quite expensive to produce, and that that was why I sought money for my time: to pay for the production of my art. This was only partially true—it was also necessary to pay for the production of my life—but clients prefer to support a starving artist than a girl buying food, clothes, and shelter. "What was so expensive about it?" he asked. "Other people's labor required to make it," I answered. It was odd to speak about labor. I couldn't tell if it bothered him or turned him on.

An hour into dinner, he handed me another envelope, containing $1,000—the two envelopes together totaling the amount I'd initially quoted him for my time. He said he wanted to give me this envelope regardless, but that clearly wasn't true. He seemed harmless enough. I figured it would behoove me to go upstairs with him, quickly fuck, and leave, so that I might maintain him as a regular client upon his visits to New York.

We went upstairs and his kissing style was immediately unnerving—he was sort of attacking my face, while also using little to no force. He was excited in a way that disgusted me—bubbly and vehement, like a child. There are certain things that are only palatable—beautiful, even—during sex if you are in love, or are with someone you could conceivably be in love with. That kind of excitement is one of them.

I moved to give him head, attempting to speed the pawing and writhing along, and he stopped me. He reached into his pocket and pulled out a bright red condom, saying something along the lines of, "Being safe is sexy." His grin was endless, maniacal. The red condom leered at me. It was flavored. I refuse to put flavored latex in my mouth. I got up to pee, rushed back to the bed, thanked him for a lovely evening, said I was "so tired," and ran out. I'd rarely left a client like that—if ever—taking the money and scurrying on my way, and I felt mildly emboldened. I imagined berating him: *You need to tell yourself you'd give me this money regardless of whether we fucked, so you can feel like I actually desire you? You need to feel magnanimous, different from all the other clients who you imagine don't care if I like it or not? You're the feminist type? Fine, prove it.* But in another way it just felt unsettling, bad. I don't like conning people, not because it's morally wrong but simply because it's stressful, unpleasant. For better or worse, I'm not a take-the-money-and-run kind of girl—or at least I thought I wasn't, until I did.

I had a similar encounter days apart—I can't remember which happened first. I met a very tall middle-aged man in a hotel lobby, we did our getting-to-know-you dance, and after about a half hour he brought up disdainfully that the way I had communicated with him prior to our meeting was too pointed and transactional—I had simply stated my social rate—as though I do this all the time, and would fuck him regardless of whether or not I liked him when I met him, as long as he paid me. All of which was, of course, true, and not something that should have surprised or upset him. He was obscenely wealthy. I told him that him acting as though I shouldn't seek compensation to meet, even just to suss out whether or not we were a chemistry match, as he wanted to do, was offensive to me: all interaction with him involved catering to his fantasies, and was therefore work. I don't mind being called a whore except in circumstances like this one where someone means it as a synonym for vile, worthless. Again, I should have left but I was determined to get more than he'd yet given me, now having sat through judgment from someone who thought he was better than me, as though his reason for being there was more human than mine.

He seemed nervous to have offended me and acted apologetic, fumbling, saying he was new at this. We walked to his nearby residence, and I asked him specifics of his sexual fantasies, hoping to learn how to most quickly and easily make more money and leave. He told me he was interested in being dominated and controlled, so I had him strip, and he begged to touch me and kiss me and I said no. I asked how much money he had in his apartment, and he answered $1,500 so I had him lead me to his briefcase, hand it to me, and then lie supine on his bed. I walked to the edge of the mattress, took off my underwear, stuffed it in his mouth, and left. I stood on the subway platform feeling strange. I wore a very short skirt, and it was inconvenient to be left without underwear. I felt accomplished, but also—I had wanted to be left with everything, and I still had given something up.

As that month came to a close—after all the work, after crying in the car, after seeing not-myself in the mirror—I wondered why I put myself in the positions I did. Did I need to? How long would I be able to withstand it? If not this, what did I want to do to make a living? I was impressed by how good I had become at sex work. I had thought of myself as a novice for so long, and now I reflected on my skill at securing money even when it felt elusive, at correctly judging the fine line between situations that were dangerous and those that were merely unpleasant. I was able to read men accurately—all of my clients have been men—and able to get payment even from those who loathed the idea of paying me. But despite the money, something was being extracted from me, too, and wildly so. I was drained. And when I thought about how much was being taken from me, in comparison to what was being taken from the men paying me—what it cost me versus what it cost them—I grew angrier still.

I sat on the beach during Art Basel 2021, talking to someone who had made his whole life in the art world. I had walked onto the sand, carrying my shoes, wearing a tiny plaid skirt and a tattered white top. I couldn't find the person I was looking for, and as I wandered around, confused, a group of teens heckled me. "Sit with us," they called out. "You're lost!" Their laughter grew louder when I found him. He kissed me on the cheek, shirtless with his swim trunks, old enough to be my father and looking even older—he was exactly twice my age. I told him we had to move away from the group; I was flustered enough as it was.

We were sort of sleeping together, sort of not. I was also working on the trip, in multiple ways—showing a film and seeing a client—and I was exhausted, wild-eyed. I had never been to Miami before. I loved the artifice of it all; at least once in every social interaction I said, "This is so *Ballers*," referring to the 2015 HBO show starring The Rock, but no one in Florida seemed to appreciate the reference. My boyfriend, with whom I'd watched the entire series, was the only one who appreciated it, so I took to texting him the phrase, though he was back in New York. The person I was meeting had Ritz-Carlton branded towels. We swam briefly—I in my underwear—and then lay down in the sun to talk.

We talked about monogamy. He was lying by omission to his partner, not telling her he'd slept with me even though he was ostensibly allowed to. He said that my work must disrupt my ability to develop truly intimate relationships. I said that he was wrong, but it was clear he didn't believe me. "How could it not?" he asked. "It's not to say sex work doesn't impact a relationship, but everything impacts a relationship. I'm a lot more honest than you," I said.

I didn't like that he said this to me, and because I didn't like it, it stayed with me. I had brought a friend on the trip—we were seeing clients together, and she was also helping me navigate the landscape, having worked in and around galleries for many years—and I told her what he'd said. She had worked with him in the past on a biennial of sorts, and was the one to introduce us in the first place. "I hope he'd say that to any artist and not just you," she said. "Say what?" I asked. "That your work could impact and disrupt your intimate relationships. That's just true of any artist, it's not a hooker thing," she said. I had never thought about it like that, and it helped. My work, in the end—my real work, my art work—is more damning to my relationships than anything else. Exposure—which my work relies upon—violates privacy and therefore, often, trust.

When I got home from that trip, I talked to my boyfriend about it—my fears around how my work would impact our relationship. Or rather, I wrote him a letter: "All of the ways I've been able to find freedom in the years we've been together—which is I think one of the main things that drives my life—have been because of you, or in partnership with you." I reflected on the way I've made much of my work, up to this point: working myself up, through my own capacity for fantasy, over scenarios I create; becoming easily intoxicated by someone's intoxication with me; eliciting a particular kind of emotional intensity from myself, played out around things and people that don't really matter, ultimately, to me. I try not to do this callously—I do it with and around people who want something from me, and who ultimately are in positions of greater power than I am, whether through financial or socio-cultural positioning, usually both. Still, it requires my focus, taking me—when I'm ensnared in a new piece—into a part of my mind that is far away from my home, and far away from my life. In her essay "Scenes from an Open Marriage," Jean Garnett writes, "I have heard the argument that true intimacy cannot exist where one partner is having any significant, preoccupying experience from which the other is excluded. Maybe there's something to that. Then again, people find all kinds of ways to be preoccupied."

He took everything in, and he said that he understood why I felt compelled to make the work I did, even if it could hurt him, or violate—as a consequence—us. He is very measured, often a rational foil to my hysterics. He feels but doesn't cry, in other words. He said that I have to make the work I have to make, and if he doesn't want to endure any of that work we would break up, because we both have to do the things we have to do, and we can both only withstand so much. It was true, and deeply kind. Years ago, I picked a drunken fight and asked him what he would do if I fucked his friend, which I didn't remember in the morning. When we fought about it again the next day and I cried, feeling like I'd broken something I didn't even remember dropping, he said that it was a good thing that I push boundaries; that I'm provocative. "But not with me," he said. "With people who you already know love you, there's no point. Don't do it with me."

My friend and mentor, the woman artist—and another person who is exactly twice my age—told me that it is possible to leave an art space, a public one, where you have produced a work, whole. "It's hard," she said, "but it is possible." She said it in the context of the first iteration of my incall pieces, sitting with me in the gallery before it opened. "Andrea Fraser had something taken from her by her gallerists," she said—namely, money. I, on the other hand, was operating outside of commercial bounds by organizing my own marketplace, giving no one a cut. "But you have had nothing taken from you, not yet. You can leave this space whole." I think about that all the time, and I still don't know if it's true.

On Legibility

Qualeasha Wood's *The [Black] Madonna/Whore Complex* is a woven and beaded cotton tapestry depicting the artist on webcam within Apple's Photo Booth application screen, wearing a dress and offering a cross and a heart, floating above early-aughts-looking text boxes that read, "are you ready?" and "young hot ebony is online." Each text box contains what look like clickable buttons that read "enter salvation." It was acquired by the Met in 2021, and the work is described on the museum's website in this way: "By presenting herself as both holy icon and object of desire, Wood rejects the racist, sexist stereotype that views Black women solely as promiscuous commodities; she accomplishes this move by enshrining and controlling her own image . . . 'If I'm going to get fetishized out here,' she says, 'I'm going to fetishize myself.'"

Wood is a digital native, born in 1996, intimately familiar with the fracturing and proliferation of the self that happens online. Her work is about seeing and being seen. In an interview with *W*, she explains,

> By centering myself in work, I know that there's a conversation around my image that's happening, whether I'm present or not. It allows me to have surveillance on other people because I'm literally watching a conversation about me . . . After I got doxxed, I just realized there is no such thing as privacy . . . so I claim consent [of my image] for

myself before it can be taken from me. I'm gaining ownership back over something that I felt was lost.

Though Wood is clothed in her self-portraits, her art uses porn search terms and camgirl marketing language in the same frame as her visage, forcing her viewers to recall how they might search for or encounter her image, or an image like hers, in their private online lives, while they encounter her image in the rarefied air of the Met. She deftly troubles legibility through context. In the same interview, she says of her work, smiling, "At their core, they're just selfies. I hate Duchamp, but I think one of the most important things was the idea of 'What is art?' It just has to be proclaimed art." I love that she says she hates Duchamp so plainly. Blunt and piercing, like a gaze, like a hammer, like the sound effect accompanying every token tip on Chaturbate.

When I began my first incall show, a man wrote to me: "I would like this to be an incredibly open, extraordinarily frank and open transactional arrangement where the art is commissioned like art, as it should be," he said. "With no flirting or unspoken limits or desires. For example, a detailed schedule or program for say 5 hours? In 15 minute increments. I agree with your premise. It is correct. Let's take transactional intimacy to its farthest possible boundary." The listed commission fee—on both the gallery's website, and the Eros ad I'd placed and paid for out of the gallery's production budget—was $20,000, chosen in reference to Andrea Fraser's work. He provided the standard screening information—legal name, verification of the employment he claimed—and we set to planning.

I was surprised at someone taking my invitation to commission seriously, in the context of performance—I expected potential clients to see the wink and the nod for what it was, window dressing for an otherwise standard relation. But here was someone who wanted a *program.* My first thought was that I could not provide a program for legal reasons. I couldn't write out specific sex acts I would agree to be commissioned for, which is what I imagined he meant. I wrote back,

> I will need to learn about your desires, fantasies, and limits before creating the work. We will discuss terms on an end-to-end encrypted platform, or over the phone, or in person. If you require a written, 15-minute-incremented program, there are two options: hand delivery by me, and I will burn the document after you peruse it; or, an encrypted document sent digitally, that will self-destruct within an allotted time. Again, no record of the performance itself can exist, save memory and certificate of ownership.

He obliged. The date of our scheduled phone call arrived, and he canceled at the last moment, citing "unexpected medical tests." He sent me $3,000 digitally and abandoned his will to participate.

I had a client whose friend was a blue-chip gallerist, and he introduced me to that friend via email, asking the gallerist to look at my work.

This client was the kind who wanted to mentor me, and he mentioned his connection to this person as soon as he found out I was an artist. He dangled the possibility of setting us up for a studio visit during our appointments, and I encouraged him to, in part out of curiosity over whether or not he would actually do it. The gallerist was friends, also, with my client's wife, and though my client would present me as someone he knew through a more standard type of work, I felt sure my art itself would give him away.

After telling me he wouldn't, in fact, provide an introduction, he changed his mind—I don't know why—and texted, "What email should I use for you?" I sent the gallerist links to my visual work and reviews of my conceptual work, despite knowing that this kind of forced audience never leads to much. He responded, spelling my name wrong: "I think you need to focus on what is authentic in your work, the style of filmmaking you are working on is elegant but has been done many times before. What is your original language?" I didn't begrudge him for his lack of interest in my work—taste is staunchly personal, after all—but I did for his advice, patronizing as it was. Given that it was couched in a question of authenticity, he seemed to be calling me a whore, rather than an artist. An *elegant* one, but a whore nonetheless. I thought about the supercilious question for weeks: What is your original language?

I imagined him jerking off to the video I'd sent him. I imagined Venmo-requesting him. I imagined writing back that my original language was fucking, though that's not true; it was drawing, and then writing. I imagined how much he wanted to fuck me, which gave me a certain kind of power, but not much. I imagined his rejection of me as a rejection of his friend who was clearly hiring prostitutes. I imagined myself as a casualty of his disapproval, or fear or jealousy masked as disapproval, which was more likely. I imagined that he didn't think there could be anything authentic in the work of a woman who priced her pussy, and he wasn't wrong, but he was wrong to find authenticity compelling. Artifice is compelling, which upsets people to admit, especially men. I said, "Thanks so much; I look forward to our paths crossing in the future!" which felt as bitchy as I could get away with.

The next time I saw him, my client and I talked about the commercialism of Damien Hirst, and I realized I no longer reviled it as I used to; in a way, I admired it. Allegedly Hirst once said, before he was famous, "I can't wait to get into a position to make really bad art and get away with it." Again, taste is individual; I think the art he found his original success with was *really bad*. Nonetheless, it's an honest position to take: it's repulsive to have to pretend gallery executives champion and decry work based on what is good, or authentic, or new, as opposed to what is profitable. What is good or authentic or new might align, in any given moment, with what is profitable—but the latter will always trump the former.

I write confessionally because it is the way I know how to write. I came up during "the personal-essay boom"—a pinnacle moment for the proliferation of overwritten, underpaid, trauma-ridden personal stories across the internet—coined as such by *New Yorker* columnist Jia Tolentino in her oft-cited 2017 piece on the fad:

> The commodification of personal experience was also women's territory: the small budgets of popular women-focussed Web sites, and the rapidly changing conventions and constrictions surrounding women's lives, insured it. And so many women wrote about the most difficult things that had ever happened to them and received not much in return. Most sites paid a few hundred dollars for such pieces at most; xoJane paid fifty dollars. When I began writing on the Internet, I wrote personal essays for free.

I began thinking about writing publicly during this time, and I'm sure what I read shaped what I thought I could get paid to write about. I read personal essays constantly. Some I liked. A lot I found stupid, or exploitative, but still engrossing. Indeed, *xoJane* published, in 2015, an anonymous entry in their infamous well of staggering overshares: "IT HAPPENED TO ME: I Was an

Escort for Eight Years, Believing It Would Empower Me, and It Didn't." Presumably, the author was paid $50 for her piece.

The personal essay boom responded to our moment's demand for the confessional from cultural producers, which is a fucked-up state of affairs for many reasons. Such a ravenous appetite for the extraction and consumption of others' shock- or deviant- or trauma-inflected stories mirrors and normalizes the privacy-less, personal-data-driven dystopian corporate empire we live under. But: I do not believe the erotic and the intellectual must be separated, and I am curious to cross and recross the boundary between the politicized reader and the voyeur, the ally and the client, the whore and the writer.

It's true that in the creative landscape dictated by internet clickbait and self-promotion on social media, confessional writing and art is expected of people with any sort of marginal identity—and it is possible, due to my participation in a criminalized form of work, for me to be viewed as such, though I'm not, in fact, marginalized in any way. But arts spaces and publishers could see me as precarious and therefore be inclined to give me a voice. The consumer demand seems to go: if you're a sex worker, you should write about being a sex worker; if you're Black, you should write about being Black; if you're disabled, you should write about being disabled; if you're, at the least, a woman, you should write about being a woman. Neither these demands, nor the consequences of denying or fulfilling them, are meted out uniformly: white writers and artists on the left gain platforms and credibility in leaning on any marginalized aspects of their identities and can opt in and out of these identities at will, enjoying different forms of legibility in different spaces. Writers of color can't opt out and often aren't assigned pieces beyond identity politics, particularly if they do not also have the right socioeconomic or academic background.

Many meaningfully resist this tokenization and its imperative to self-extract. In his introduction letter to *Art in America's* May 2021 New Talent Issue, which he guest edited and filled with "an international mix of Black writers, critics, curators, and artists," curator Antwaun Sargent writes,

> Today's arts coverage is dominated by a group of critics who are mostly white and non-Black people of color. The most celebrated Black art writers tend to be academics, which creates the impression that Black writers, unlike their white and non-Black POC counterparts, need a PhD to contribute to the discourse. These white and non-Black POC writers have started discussing "overlooked" Black artists and cultural figures. I ask, "overlooked" by whom? For decades, we've been reading the same few white critics, who hold coveted editorial posts at widely read outlets, and few if any have publicly acknowledged their own acts of erasure. Their articles about Blackness have contributed to a hyper-focus on Black art that deals with social issues alone; prioritizing this genre above all else continues that legacy of overlooking.

It can be radical, effective, or simply thoughtful to withstand this pressure, if one is a person who, possessing a certain identity, is told that trauma-mining is their only valuable cultural contribution. This has produced a fetish of the lived experience, lauded by media and marketplace alike. Case in point: some of the work Qualeasha Wood makes she'll never show the public. She explains, "Unfortunately, as a person of color, trauma is what sells. I live and exist beyond that, and my work should too," and further warns students, "You need to lay it all out and then bury it carefully."

For a time, mainstream culture had little appetite for writing or art by sex workers that did not paint the work in an exploitative and traumatic light, or that was not simply salacious memoir. Responding to such ceaseless requests in their introduction to *Revolting Prostitutes*, British sex workers and activists Juno Mac and Molly Smith write, "Despite the expectation that sex workers will 'tell our stories,' this is not a memoir and we will not be sharing any sexy escapades." Similarly, in *Playing the Whore*—a largely theoretical text—Melissa Gira Grant writes, "This is not a peep show. So I will not, for example, be telling my story, though the means by which I came to the story I am telling here is inseparable from my experience as a sex worker." In an interview on the publication of her poetry collection drawing from years of escort work, Rachel Rabbit White laments,

> Women and authors of color or other marginalized people are often asked, under the guise of authenticity, to burst that bubble of safety. When I first read some of these poems in a more academic workshop, many suggested I open with my sex work "credentials." They didn't know if they could believe me, so they asked me to out myself and make myself vulnerable before they could read me.

Mac, Smith, Gira Grant, and Rabbit White are all white. It's worth noting that the demand for authenticity they are all responding to not only produces particular kinds of speech at the expense of others, but also effectively forecloses the speech of those who cannot or do not publicly identify as sex workers. And it's worth noting, too, that the demand to tell one's story, and thus prove one's authenticity, goes beyond an external cultural expectation and has been adapted into factions of the sex workers' rights movement, part and parcel of both online and in-person monitoring of who gets to speak on sex work. Telling one's story is akin to representation—mainstream opportunities dangled to those on the margins alongside a promise that a particular kind of speech or media will lead to change in the conditions that marginalized them in the first place.

Nowadays, when a bad take on sex work makes the rounds on Twitter, or a celebrity or influencer dabbles in OnlyFans or softcore porn production, or a popular singer borrows the aesthetics of stripping or hooking for a music video, sex workers inevitably post criticisms and write articles railing the person in question for invoking sex work and its deviant cultural capital without being a real sex worker. This focus on what makes a person a real or actual sex worker implies that a kind of authenticity—one that could only be satisfied by a person publicly disclosing all of their sex work experiences, a compulsion that for many could lead to violence, criminalization, or deportation—would make their art or article better, or legitimate, or just *okay*, even if it is actually bad. Participation in a certain type of labor is not enough to assume political affinity or solidarity. When I see someone questioning whether or not a person with an opinion on sex work has ever sold sex, my first thought now is—who cares? But these questions highlight the current conditions structuring discourse around sex, labor, and capitalism: the confession authenticates the speaker, rendering her legible, and thus, consumable.

In an interview titled "The Ideal Neoliberal Subject Is the Subject of Trauma," queer theorist Yasmin Nair discusses the demand for authentication-through-trauma that permeates current discourse on consent and rape culture, as well as larger critiques of patriarchy, capitalism, and immigration: "You cannot speak about capitalism as a person of color if you are not willing to talk about yourself as a trauma subject, or at least as someone who's afflicted by capitalism, as opposed to someone who is an analyst of capitalism." Nair is concerned that "the imperative to confess, and . . . to reveal oneself as the wounded subject" derails analysis of the socio-political conditions that facilitate state-based and interpersonal violence. She elaborates, "There's a kind of demand for authenticity in all of this that I find particularly vexing. And I know for a fact that many people who have a critique of trauma and of violence and of the state may well have been sexually abused, but just don't talk about it. And does that make them less authentic?" In an essay published on their Patreon, "A Question of Authenticity," moses moon writes,

> Am I a real artist? Does my identity as a creative change how I engage sex work (politics)? Does poverty? . . . I'm wondering what it means to be pursuing sex work as a means to an end. There's a long history of creatives moonlighting as whores or in related professions in order to achieve their goal of making their creative work their main source of income. Does my experience matter? Should I abandon my writing in favor of pursuing erotic labor vis-à-vis authenticity?

I have similarly wondered about the feedback-loop relationship between the tradition of funding creative work through sex work, and then the decision to create art publicly *about* sex work. Is this a capitulation to the kind of writing and art society most likes to extract from women artists? I wonder if there exists a circular internalization of misogyny in this choice: that girls are taught to see their value in sex, so monetize it, thinking they've beaten the system—but ultimately their value-through-sex is simply reinforced, so they begin to see their creative value in that vein, too. We might pursue sex work to support an art practice that is allegedly, at first, independent of sex work, but it often becomes inextricably linked to or entirely about it. In other words, by internalizing the idea that all we have to sell is sex, it also happens that what a lot of us end up creating, or creating about, is, in one form or another, sex.

moon, though, further critiqued the uneven impact of the demand for authenticity, this time on a Twitter thread:

> I'm trying to wrap my mind around how fucked up you have to be to be a childless, thin, conventionally attractive student claiming that another sex worker is inauthentic or "posing" because their labor isn't accessible TO YOU? . . . Weaponization of identity politics. Hyperfocus on determining authenticity. [Authenticity] as social currency. Social media as performance . . . For the record, the most prominent & highly followed sex workers who are considered "public figures" on [Twitter] are nonblack women who usually fall into the middle to high income category. Think about that and then ask why an impoverished black SWer/artist has to prove authenticity.

moon's attack on the racist and classist pressures to prove oneself as authentic in order to be seen as a valid discursive contributor, along with their strategic resistance and acquiescence to such pressures on their own terms, is a choreography that disrupts intra-industry demands on poor, part-time, non-professionalized, or non-white sex workers to make their working lives legible to hyper-professionalized, mostly white, high-earning, and full-time sex workers. It also challenges extra-industry demands on these same sex workers to provide trauma porn and autobiographical-erotic fodder to the entertainment industry, the white savior industry, lawmakers, and voyeuristic civilians alike.

To add to all this, the circumstances surrounding sex work discourse in the United States, and certainly in New York, where I work and live and write, have changed in the last few years. In April 2021, the Manhattan district attorney's office announced it would no longer prosecute prostitution, with district attorney Cyrus R. Vance Jr. elaborating, "Criminally prosecuting prostitution does not make us safer, and too often, achieves the opposite result by further marginalizing vulnerable New Yorkers." The office would continue to prosecute people patronizing sex workers, expressing tacit support for the Nordic model, wherein sex workers are decriminalized but clients are not. This is an insufficient model; criminalized clients fear arrest and exposure and are therefore less likely to comply with screening methods sex workers use to stay safe, hesitant to share their information lest it reach the wrong hands in a sting or raid. The "Sex Trade Survivors Justice and Equality Act," a bill introduced in the New York state legislature in 2021, supports this partial decriminalization model, while another bill, the "Stop Violence in the Sex Trades Act," first introduced to the legislature in 2019, proposes full decriminalization. The two bills and their supporters remain engaged in a divisive ideological battle.

Nonetheless, full decriminalization has at least entered mainstream debate, and myriad books, articles, television shows, and movies that portray sex workers—particularly those who are white and high-earning—as complex, multifaceted individuals have entered the public lexicon. The white, high-end sex worker can speak freely on whatever she likes, precisely because she isn't, at first glance, assumed to be a hooker, or assumed to only be a hooker, or to be a disempowered hooker. At this point in the cultural conversation, contrary to those who have written previously on the topic—and in no small part because of their contributions and their refusals to mine their own experiences—I think it would be ridiculous to imply that I feel an exploitative demand to write from a personal standpoint or to mine any suffering that I may or may not have experienced. So why, then, confess, if it's precisely what others have worked so hard to avoid?

Years ago, I was in bed with a man who hired me, and it became clear he wanted to have unprotected sex. He rubbed against me, murmuring deflections to my suggestion that he get up and get a condom, as I physically but nearly imperceptibly resisted, still kissing him as I lightly pressed my thighs together, angling myself, ever softly, away. I wasn't scared, though he was over me, and much stronger than me, and I did not know him at all save for his legal name and his place of employment. He didn't seem like the type of man who would actually rape me, just the type of man who would push his luck. When I finally became concerned that he would soon push inside of me despite my increasingly clear physical cues not to, I spoke. I explained plainly that we would not be having sex without a condom but that I'd be happy to do something else. He protested mildly—"Even if I don't come inside of you?"—and then relented, retrieving protection.

At the time, I found this experience interesting: a way to think about power dynamics as they relate to client and hooker, men and women, having sex with strangers. *Why hadn't I felt threatened, and why hadn't I asserted myself earlier?* I wondered, with the forced intellectual remove of an anthropologist. Months afterward, it dawned on me: enduring a man's efforts to push my boundaries is commonplace and boring, just like working to live. But taking pains to find such violations interesting, as opposed to alarming or disappointing, gives us a way to live within them more easily, letting them linger in only certain parts of the mind.

The same is true of confessional writing. Bowing to the creative moment that I'm both willingly and forcibly part of makes it bearable, livable. Performing intimacy is also work I know how to do: the studied reveal is the specialty of the whore. Guy Debord writes, "The spectacle is the stage at which the commodity has succeeded in totally colonizing social life. Commodification is not only visible, we no longer see anything else; the world we see is the world of the commodity." Our desires are not our own; what we find worthwhile does not come from ourselves. In *Stepford Wives*, the lobotomized, robot-ized women serve as ATMs as well as housewives. When I open my mouth, I wish money would come out. Tiqqun writes, "The appalling thing isn't that the Young-Girl is fundamentally a whore, but that she refuses to perceive herself as such." Well, here I am!

I wish participation in late capitalism on no one; it's a horrifying state of affairs. But if I must participate—and I must, as a person who needs to earn money in order to live—I've always found it more interesting to search for modes of scam and subversion while offering myself up wholly to capital's insidious demands, than to refuse. This is what, in part, drew me to sex work; this is what, in part, drew me to writing about it.

A discursive change around sex work occurred in the nineteenth century—a century in which language about work took on more particular and heightened meanings in the face of mass political changes. Chief among them was the abolition of slavery in the United States and Europe, which led to a restructuring of the language that defined labor, servitude, freedom, and incarceration such that an enslaved Black workforce could still legally exist. Previously undefined social and labor roles, now concretized, emerged from these conditions and tortured definitions.

Melissa Gira Grant writes that where previously there had been no one word for a woman who sells sex—at the time, *whore* denoted simply an unrespectable woman or adulterer—now the word *prostitute* emerged, to be "applied to a much older set of practices, and . . . to produce a person by transforming a behavior (however occasional) into an identity." Around the same time, arguably, the figure of the *starving artist* emerged—a worker identified precisely by his lack of income. Critic William Deresiewicz writes,

> As traditional beliefs broke down across the 18th and 19th centuries, art inherited the role of faith . . . As with art, so with artists, the new priests and prophets. It was modernity that gave us the bohemian, the starving artist, and the solitary genius, images respectively of blissful unconventionality, monkish devotion, and spiritual election. Artistic poverty was seen as glamorous, an outward sign of inner purity.

The imaginaries call forth a figure defined by either her callous selling of self, or his ascetic refusal to sell.

The whore is a woman; the artist is a man; and neither, until the 1970s, is a worker. In her research article "Dirty Commerce: Art Work and Sex Work since the 1970s," Julia Bryan-Wilson explores the simultaneous movements of art workers and sex workers to gain recognition as *workers*. She writes,

> The corralling of these incongruent identities under the sign of work signals the unhinging of previous class positions. It might be that, as the coherence of worker fractured, the category became more available for downward appropriation by the likes of artists (who, due to cultural capital and educational privilege, sit above the working class) as well as aspirational renaming by the (generally understood to be lumpen) prostitute.

What makes sex work *work* is that most people who do it need the money. What makes art work, arguably, not *work*, is that most people who find themselves able to do it full-time—even find themselves making money at it—do not, in fact, need the money.

In 1964, conceptual artist Robert Morris performed *Site*, alongside Carolee Schneemann, whom he had enlisted to reenact the scene depicted in Édouard Manet's famous 1863 painting *Olympia*. In the painting, a naked, white prostitute wearing a flower in her hair, a ribbon around her neck, pearls in her ears, and a bangle on her wrist reclines, legs crossed, breasts bare, arm draped across her body with her hand resting on her thigh to obscure her genitals. She leans against white pillows, white sheets, and cream-colored floral linens. A Black maid, dressed in white, holds a bouquet of flowers open, over Olympia's legs. A black cat, back arched, stands at the very edge of the cot, looking agitated. The painting was controversial at the time due to Olympia's profession and direct gaze. In his reenactment, Morris, wearing work clothes and a mask of his own face fabricated by Jasper Johns, deconstructs a large wooden box, removing four-by-eight plywood sheets one at a time, revealing Schneemann inside. She reclines naked on a sheet, wearing only earrings and Olympia's black ribbon tied around her neck, signifying her harlotry. The pose, gaze, and sheets are the same. A soundtrack of construction noise—jackhammering—plays in the background. Morris returns the plywood sheets, shrouding Schneemann once again.

Writing of Morris upon his death in 2019, Schneemann recalls of their working together:

> During the presentations of *Site*, my own kinetic theater was obscured by the appreciation of and excitement around your work. I have said that being in *Site* both historicized

> and immobilized me. The fact is that it remains a visionary, transformative event that forever reshaped references to historic imagery. You cleaved the specific qualities of painting and sculpture, of movement and stillness.

Schneemann both resents and appreciates the fervor surrounding *Site*; initially, Morris's performance eclipsed her own performances and films, which often dealt with, from her perspective, her own naked body's involvement in the labor of art-making. Her work was derided as both too pornographic, the nudity gratuitous—as in her 1963 series *Eye Body*, in which she photographed herself nude, painted, with props, to which critics said, "If you want to paint, put your clothes back on"—and not pornographic enough—as in the 1969 screening of her revelatory sex film *Fuses*, which, according to the *New York Times*, disappointed "male critics" who hoped it would be more hardcore. *Fuses* captured Schneemann and her partner, James Tenney, having sex in their bed in the home they shared, from the point of view of their cat, Kitch, shot over a period of "a year or two." Schneemann said of her intention behind making the piece, "I needed to see if I could re-proportion the structures that were being given to me as hierarchical aesthetic factors. Pop art produced mechanized female bodies and I wanted to show something different from that deadness and slickness." At the time, the aesthetic hierarchy ranked work made by men using naked women's bodies significantly higher than work made by women using those same bodies. The women's work was lesser, in no small part because women artists were so maligned in the industry, period. Schneemann said she'd "been told from the earliest times that [painting] was pointless and that I should stop. At Bard my best painting professor said, 'Don't set your heart on art, you're only a girl.'"

Bryan-Wilson writes that *Site*'s "display of female flesh alongside Morris's heavy lifting . . . puts into dialogue sex work and artistic process . . . propos[ing] both its artists . . . as laborers, even as Schneemann's only work is to appear as an object." Indeed, Morris's *Site* brought two people involved in Manet's painting to life, the art worker and the sex worker, interrogating the labor of object-making and objecthood. Yet there are three people involved in this painting, three people working, not two. The Black maid holding flowers is equal in Manet's painting to a curtain or a prop, made out to be less important than even the bouquet she holds. She is disregarded by both white male artist and white female prostitute alike. The differential between the artist-man and the prostitute-woman is based on the greater differential of race, as these positions are born from a social order dependent on slavery and racial servitude. Manet's painting was created in 1863, not even two decades after the abolition of slavery in France.

White girls love to feel sorry for ourselves—to focus on arenas in which we feel denigrated or unrecognized, and to reclaim those arenas loudly. White feminists make a formal politic of it; the rest of us merely do it when it's convenient. In her 2016 essay "Closing the Loop," artist, critic, and curator Aria Dean critiques the ubiquitous selfie feminism of the early to mid-2010s, championed and lauded by largely young, white, cis, women artists and critics for "the control afforded through the act of self-imaging [that] is invaluable; nothing less, in fact, than the primary feminist tool for resistance." The movement traded on, in Dean's biting and accurate estimation, "a basic-bitch politic of visibility," whereby white girls allegedly "reclaimed" digital spaces from their male counterparts, photographing themselves rather than existing as the subjects of photographs, and showcasing aspects of cis girlhood deemed distasteful by the Male Gaze or Instagram—depending on who you were asking—body hair and period blood chief among them. This is a way of becoming Manet and Olympia both; it is also a way to refuse to see the Black maid at all.

The epigraph to Dean's piece, it turns out, comes from conceptual artist Lorraine O'Grady's seminal 1992 work of criticism, "Olympia's Maid: Reclaiming Black Female Subjectivity," in which O'Grady writes that Laura, the model Manet used to paint Olympia's maid, is "the most famous example . . . of what Judith Wilson calls 'the legions of black servants who loom in the shadows of European and European-American aristocratic portraiture.'" She describes the approximation of Laura in the painting as

> Jezebel and Mammy, prostitute and female eunuch, the two-in-one. When we're through with her inexhaustibly comforting breast, we can use her ceaselessly open cunt. And best of all, she is not a real person, only a robotic servant . . . Laura's place is outside what can be conceived of as woman. She is the chaos that must be excised, and it is her excision that stabilizes the West's construct of the female body, for the "femininity" of the white female body is ensured by assigning the not-white to a chaos safely removed from sight. Thus only the white body remains as the object of a voyeuristic, fetishizing male gaze.

Laura is not legible as a woman, not even the conditional womanhood gifted by objectification. And yet, white feminists continue to abhor the Male Gaze, as though a homogenous army of Men is gazing at a homogenous army of Women, all sexualized and objectified in the same manner.

I do not know how to speak about this, exactly, because I think to lament over and over the dehumanization of Black women, as a white woman, so too adds to that dehumanization.

But: the white girl can play the hooker, depict herself in art, gain the cultural capital, and lose little in the process. Objectification and simple sexism are not all that bad. Black women have had and continue to have a much more complicated relationship with visibility foisted upon them, to great material consequence.

In 1991 at the Sonnabend Gallery in SoHo, commodities-trader-turned-art-star Jeff Koons debuted *Made in Heaven*, a series of works depicting Koons in sexual positions with Italian porn star and politician Ilona Staller (stage name Cicciolina). Though neither spoke the other's language, the two married shortly after producing the works. Photographs printed on canvas, along with marble and glass sculptures, depicted the couple in softcore Kama Sutra poses alongside more explicit visuals. *Dirty Ejaculation* showed Koons ejaculating between Staller's open legs.

At the time, reviewers focused on the distinction between artwork and pornography: novelist and critic Jim Lewis wrote, "[the work is] not . . . pornographic . . . because an art work becomes prurient only when it ceases to be a representation of desire and instead becomes the impetus for it . . . These works would be very much diminished if they provided occasions for arousal. They don't, and they're not intended to." Koons himself made the distinction less absolute, telling *Vanity Fair* the pieces were "advertising for a porno film I'm going to make with Cicciolina," that, with respect to sex acts, would include "everything." In the same interview, he praised his wife as an artist in her own right, explaining, "Ilona uses her body in the way another artist uses a paintbrush or a chisel. She uses her genitalia. And she communicates a very precise language with her genitalia." In 1997 Koons sold *Ilona On Top* on auction at Sotheby's for $140,000, later selling other pieces of the series for close to a million.

By 1994, Koons and Staller were embroiled in an acrimonious divorce and custody battle for their toddler, Ludwig. In the proceedings, Koons sought to use Staller's career as an adult film star against her, telling the court, "To have a family based on Protestant values was important to me." The *New Yorker* reported on his damning comments: "He berated her pornographic work as 'vile' and 'vulgar' . . . he declared, 'She'll do anything to dismantle cultural mores.'" Koons and his attorney thought the court might be swayed by getting "a picture of what's involved," promptly turning out the lights to screen clips from Staller's films, in which she had sex with a snake, had sex with three men at once, and had sex with "a fat man in a field." Lauding Staller's films as on par with high art just three years prior, and going on record in a prestige publication that he intended to make hardcore films with her—that, indeed, what he thought about as they posed for photos together was "having anal sex with Ilona"—Koons now pivoted to the long tradition of using a woman's participation in sex work to render her an unfit mother in the eyes of the law. The court granted him custody.

In a 2013 interview with Pharrell Williams on the musician-cum-entrepreneur's Reserve Channel show *ARTST TLK*, Jeff Koons describes his relationship to his work as "trying to share . . . transcendence with the viewer: I believe very much in the beholder's share . . . that an artwork is completed in the viewer. The object is just some kind of transponder." The beholder's share is a concept coined by Alois Riegl, nineteenth-century art historian of the Vienna School, and subsequently popularized by his disciples Ernst Kris and Ernst Gombrich; simply, "that art is incomplete without the perceptual and emotional involvement of the viewer." (The beholder's share might also be a way to describe prostitution: such a relation requires a perceptual involvement of the viewer and could be said to culminate in their involvement.)

Koons evokes this idea while reflecting on his decision to create and subsequently destroy much of the *Made in Heaven* series. He tells Williams,

> I wanted to make a body of work that would help remove that kind of guilt and shame, and so the intentions of the work are very good. So even though it's very direct, and some of the images are kind of explicit, there's a place for adults to look at those type of images, and to be involved with that dialogue.

Pharrell responds, "I think context is everything." As Koons goes on to describe Staller as having "no guilt about her body . . . no shame about her body, and so she was able to present that very clearly," a naked woman walks up to the two and pours them water. She is expressionless. The show airs on safe-for-work channels, so her breasts and pussy are blurred out, much the way escorts sometimes blur their faces on advertising sites, or blur nipples or genitalia on social media platforms like Twitter. (Where once nudity ran free on Twitter, explicit imagery will now get one shadowbanned—hidden from discovery in the search toolbar—if not altogether suspended.) Williams neither looks at nor acknowledges her, while Koons attempts to appear unfazed. He smiles at her, though he seems unable to answer the next question until she walks away.

A naked woman serving water appears on multiple episodes of *ARTST TLK*. I could find little media commentary on what amounts to a tired aesthetic choice, except a *Forbes* article in which the reporter explains,

I'm told (often with a note of dismissive acceptance) that parading a nude female around the set is standard on Pharrell's chat show, ARTST TLK. 'Oh, that's just what he does,' seems to be the sentiment. But still, it's a transgressive moment, bait-and-switching the dignified definition of adult with the tawdry one. Without warning, Pharrell jolts us out of heady conversation and drops us into the world of meaningless eye-candy, effectively cheapening the whole interview.

The naked, servile woman seems a logical extension of music video girls: props to create a particular atmosphere, that of indulgence and provocation. For the duration of the show, Williams interviewed almost exclusively men.

Does meaningless eye candy cheapen the whole interview? One might argue that the interview was relatively cheap to begin with, as in, intellectually bereft—Koons and Williams trading platitudes about transcendence and beauty, engaging in mutual verbal masturbation. But the money in the room is palpable. Exact net worth is difficult to ascertain, but it's enough to know both artists have bought homes for roughly $30 million. (Google has Williams's net worth at $200 million, and Koons's at twice that.) What they are discussing, too, are objects as stand-ins for money, which is the mode in which Koons's art functions best.

As Williams says, context is, indeed, everything, and the point of the nude woman seems to be precisely that she is out of context. What could easily be pornographic if hosted by a different website is, in the context of an art talk: edgy, interesting, transgressive, boundary-pushing. What occurs is actually so popular a sexual fantasy that it has its own porn category: CMNF, or Clothed Male Nude Female. Koons's *Made in Heaven* pieces were, too, defined by context. David

Littlejohn covered Koons's 1992 retrospective at the San Francisco Museum of Modern Art, citing a placard at the entrance of the gallery housing the controversial pieces, which warned viewers "that these images are not pornographic because 'they do not invite the *participation* of the viewer,' [Littlejohn's emphasis] and because they show real, identifiable, nonfantasy people (who are, indeed, married)." But for all the hemming and hawing of what makes something art versus pornography, the answer is simple: the sale price. Art is just more expensive.

A few years back, the Leslie-Lohman Museum of Art hosted an exhibition titled *On Our Backs: The Revolutionary Art of Queer Sex Work*. My friend was commissioned to write about the show, and when she went to see it, she posted photos to her Instagram story of several of the pieces. Her account was immediately deleted for hosting content that went against the platform's terms of service. Eventually, after public outcry and an influx of messages to Instagram support, it was reinstated.

The group show featured the work of Shawné Michaelain Holloway, a digital and performance artist who straddles the sex and art industries, and who likes to play with power. Early in her career, she explained that all of her work serves to "carefully detail/describe one Black gURL's #identity + xxxperience of sex and pop culture online." Of the piece on view, *a personal project (2012–)*, Tiana Reid writes,

> Holloway edited videos and photographs she originally made for the amateur porn website Xtube into a glitchy, but not illegible video. On her website, she describes her time on Xtube as part of a social experiment, an investigation into power dynamics. She writes, "I use these people online just as much as they're using me," highlighting how

> sex can often be transactional even when no money is exchanged.

Holloway's work exists in a variety of contexts, by virtue of her own doing. In an interview for *The Quietus*, Allan Gardner asked her if she chose to host "a personal project" on Xtube simply because it was her only option—because "community guidelines" on any other platform might ban it. She answered that it wasn't a practical but an intentional decision:

> I hosted it there partially because I don't feel that its [sic] right to just scoop from the community and then run away with the content. Appropriation, even if I'm appropriating from a position of privilege (that I don't necessarily have in those communities) still felt disingenuous to me. Like i'm running off with your secrets. I wanted to emphasise "I am here with you guys, this is my life, so let's just play."

Unlike various predecessors, Holloway does not run from the context in which her work was created or might normally be viewed. She is an artist, and also, she is not *not* a camgirl.

I used to fear the impact of making porn in a way I didn't fear the impact of any other form of sex work. Indeed, in an essay titled "Once You Have Made Pornography," Lorelei Lee warns, "This job is not forgettable. Once you have done it, anyone who knows you have done it sees a mark on you—believes there is a thing about your personality or life history that is revealed." If everyone could see my pussy on the internet, what would it say about me? As soon as I was recognized publicly as an artist, my fear waned. I created a context in which any pornography I made could be inflected differently, readymade to be viewed or analyzed through a respectable, institutional lens. I am ashamed that I feel this way, but I do.

I decided to shoot self-portraits at the Kew Motor Inn, one of the last remaining hourly motels in New York City. The rooms are themed, ranging from innocuous, syrupy motifs like *Love Nest* and *Fantasia* to the more exoticized and offensive *Oriental Delight* and *Arabian Nights*. My favorite was *New York Skyline*.

When my friend and I went to scout the location, we checked in behind a client and the escort he'd hired; their presence at such a motel during lunchtime hours, combined with her heels and their thirty-year age gap, gave them away. We got into a room and I stripped down to the lace bodysuit I was wearing, jumping on the bed. She took photos of me, capturing my reflection in the mirrored ceiling. I grabbed her phone to take a selfie, holding it high above my head, my black-clad body and pink tongue popping against the maroon, paisley-printed comforter. A room or two away, we heard exaggerated screams, accompanied by a squeaking bed. This seemed characteristic of a seedy motel: hourly rooms promised cheap, quick access, but no veil through which to pretend what was happening wasn't happening. The room dripped of fast, sold sex; the knowledge that if you looked closely you'd find traces of those who came here before made it feel like one large effervescent come stain, an atmospheric glow.

I returned a few weeks later with my boyfriend and a photographer I hired to assist in the self-portraiture. She shot on medium format film and had experience photographing beautiful smut. The rooms were perfectly sun-dappled. I posed in various positions on the bed, on a chair, in a windowsill. I sat on the dirty mantle in front of the blue neon skyline in the New York room.

The light faded, and we moved to capture the shot I really wanted: the money shot, the facial. The moment of ejaculation has been colloquially renamed the money shot because, historically, porn producers have had to pay more for it. Citing

Marcuse and Debord, Linda Williams writes in her book *Hard Core*, "As the industry's slang term for the moment the hard-core film 'delivers the goods' of sexual pleasure, the money shot seems the perfect embodiment of the illusory and insubstantial 'one-dimensional' 'society of the spectacle' of advanced capitalism—that is, a society that consumes images even more avidly than it consumes objects." But I disagree with Williams's characterization: the money shot is neither illusory nor insubstantial. It is a photo-realistic representation of a moment of ecstasy, which is rather godly.

The photographer lit us and stood nearby while I gave my boyfriend head, my own head perched uncomfortably in such a way that it was slightly lolling off the bed, wanting to be in position for the photograph I'd instructed them to capture. He warned me he was going to come, and then he did it, streaming over my face in two perfect lines, spreading outward from my mouth like brooks feeding into a lake.

I modeled this photograph after *Exaltation*, one of Koons's photographs from *Made in Heaven*. The photo depicts Cicciolina on her back; it's a close-up of her face, with the top of her chest and neck visible. A hard, red dick rests on her tongue, with ejaculate dripping down her cheek and chin. She wears cotton-candy-colored eye makeup—blue mascara—and her eyebrows are thick and filled in, auburn-brown in shocking contrast to her bleached hair. On her head is a pearl tiara, and in her ears, costume earrings that look like clip-ons. Her clothing is seafoam. She looks like a princess, and also a little bit like she's dead. I think the piece is gorgeous; a perfect depiction of woman-as-object. I wanted to recapture it with the whore in the artist position. I wanted to see how that subject positioning might change, or not change, someone's perception of a work that was otherwise formally and compositionally the same. I was both subject and (directorial) photographer. It was my shot to solicit, and to, in several different senses, take.

I showed a series of these three photos at a gallery in Brooklyn, all capturing the extended moment of my boyfriend ejaculating onto my face. I called the series *Exalted*, changing the noun to an adjective. I did this because I don't think the facial creates a state of being, so much as it adorns one, comments on one. The face, waiting for the come shot, is already exalted—purely beautiful, waiting to be desecrated. The woman doesn't need a face of spilled milk to become more object than woman, holier than thou—she simply needs to be anticipating the moment, ready for it.

A woman came to the gallery, a lesbian who told me her marriage had been sexless for twelve years, her wife frigid. She spoke to me about intimate details of her life for forty-five minutes, divulging more than I could have even thought to ask, before turning abruptly to the photographs on the wall, remarking, "These don't look like you." I was taken aback; to me, they do. She asked if they were accurate to how I imagine myself looking when I work, and I said they were: like a painting; like a fallen angel; like a pre-Raphaelite drowned girl-child.

My friend asked me to read at the launch of their new magazine; I agreed, saying I would decide the content day-of. That morning, I texted them, "I think I'm gonna read something about how I look really beautiful when I give head." When you give head, your face shines. It shines with your own spit, and your eyes shine, tearing up while you choke.

In 2000, Taschen published Natacha Merritt's *Digital Diaries*, comprised of Merritt's pornographic photos of herself and her real-life lovers having sex, masturbating, and tying one another up. In interviews at the time, twenty-two-year-old Merritt embraced her critics, refusing to even call herself an artist, saying, "Am I a narcissist? Absolutely. It's all about me, me, me. Why is it bad to love yourself? Who taught us that?" Reviewing her work for *Salon*, David Bowman wrote,

> Merritt's blow job pictures are the most memorable images in the book because, I believe, it's unprecedented for a woman to take self-portraits depicting herself as a cocksucker . . . there is one photograph in particular (on Page 66) that is haunting somehow. Most of Merritt's face is in the frame, as well as the member that is halfway up her yap . . . In the photo, Merritt is looking up and a bit to the right, concentrating on something. After I talked with her, I knew what she was looking at.

What she was looking at, it turns out, was the monitor of her digital camera; looking at herself, her portrait half-shrouded by dick, tied-up scrotum, and her own hair falling in front of her face, waiting to see the image she wants on the screen, and then capturing that. In this way, her camera itself is a presence in her work; or rather, she takes no pains to hide the intrusion of a recording device, blurring her sex life and her art work together. In an interview printed in *Digital Diaries*, Eric Kroll asked the artist, "Which comes first—sex or photography?" She answered, "I can't separate them . . . I can't just do one without thinking about the other."

Paul Mpagi Sepuya has also, and more recently, photographed himself "as a cocksucker." In *Darkroom Mirror (_2060403)*, he appears, camera in hand, bare-chested, head turned slightly to his right. A white cock is in his mouth, a sliver of the thighs and stomach of its owner visible at the edge of the frame. To his other side, another erect, white cock appears, its head invisible behind Sepuya's own. The torso and hands of this person are partly visible at the frame's other edge. The background is black. *Art in America* described the work in Sepuya's 2019 show *The Conditions* as having "an almost religious aura." Sepuya's focus is as much on the making of an image as it is on the image itself; like Merritt's embrace of self-portraiture, Sepuya is disinterested in tricks that would render his tools invisible. He is interested in showing the mirror's stains and smudges and his own handiwork with his camera; interested in what these traces of the work's production might indicate about the movement before and after the photo, about the subjects of his photos, most of whom are friends or lovers—even if the indication is simply of their presence. His appreciation of such traces is a mode of foregrounding Blackness and queerness in his erotic work:

> To make visible a lot of these latent indexical traces requires thinking about Blackness—the material within the studio construction, or the body itself, or the camera—that those fundamentals of the medium itself, the uses of the tools, the surfaces that make visibility or invisibility possible, that they cannot be separated from a Black body, Blackness as material. But also, the ways in which that language of darkness—the dark room, the queer dark room—all kind of collapsed together, can then hopefully make those subjects inseparable from photography itself.

What brings Merritt's and Sepuya's work together is that both hinge on self-objectification, though Merritt's gaze is apolitical, while Sepuya's is explicitly political.

I appreciate that Merritt is upfront about her own self-objectification, does not take the easy way out by claiming it as a political stance—claiming that she is weaponizing the female gaze, or sexualizing her own image as a response to the culture's misogynistic fetishization of women's bodies. Any such claim would fall flat, empty. She is a thin, conventionally hot, cis white girl. If she created her content within the porn industry, her various identities would afford her opportunities to command the highest attainable rates. She is obsessed with herself, which, if neither particularly admirable nor thought-provoking, is, at the very least, honest. I think she's aesthetically brilliant, her work pre-dating the grainy aesthetic now ubiquitous on cell phone cameras and OnlyFans.

Sepuya's gaze *is* political in that he seeks to make Blackness and queerness, often erased from fine art traditions as canonized by museums and galleries, inseparable from the genre of portrait photography. He, too, is aesthetically brilliant, expertly employing metaphor, fragmentation, and pose to discomfit and arouse the viewer simultaneously. Though he takes his work seriously, he is not precious about its existence in different spaces, not worried that it might call up different, lowbrow responses. Interviewing Sepuya, the photographer Giancarlo Montes Santangelo offered up a playful anecdote: "I spotted one of your photographs on Scruff! I chatted with the guy but have no idea what his name is. I thought you'd appreciate the afterlife of the picture. It's telling though, the images and the relationships they bind are slippery." Sepuya appreciated this repurposing of his work from the gallery to the gay hook-up app: "Ah I love that story. It happens a lot . . . I've heard stories of friends being across various continents and [initiating] conversations (both in person and on apps) based on recognition from the photographs."

Artists like Sepuya and Merritt make the boundaries between the gallery and the hook-up app, the coffee table book and the smut site, slippery indeed. And the boundaries between facilitating a casual hook-up on the app and facilitating paid sex are slippery, too: in June 2021, a public outcry exploded on social media when it appeared that Apple might remove Grindr and Scruff from their app store, casualties of a new ban on apps that allow "overtly sexual or pornographic material" in the store, defined as "explicit descriptions or displays of sexual organs or activities intended to stimulate erotic rather than aesthetic or emotional feelings, and including 'hookup' apps that may include pornography or be used to facilitate prostitution." Though Apple quickly clarified that the beloved apps were safe—for now—in spite of their facilitation of nudes-trading, and though Scruff itself explicitly bans "advertising massage or escort services"—I certainly know people who trick on this app, and you certainly do, too.

In 2017, a Canadian man, on his way to visit his boyfriend in the United States, was stopped by US Customs and Border Patrol at the Vancouver Airport and interrogated. Selected for a secondary inspection while going through preclearance, he gave up his phone password and his computer to the questioning officer. The officer questioned him about an email address attached to a Craigslist account that communicated about sex ads, and then read his Scruff messages, finding one in which the man said he was "looking for loads." Though this is a well-known colloquialism for ejaculation, the officer used the message as evidence the man was soliciting sex for money—i.e., for "loads of money." The man was not allowed through the border and, on his next attempt to enter the United States, was again flagged and stopped, his phone and computer searched using the passwords customs already had saved from their previous seizure. Again, the customs officer would not let him through: "I had nude photos of myself on my phone, and they were questioning who this person was. It was really humiliating and embarrassing . . . He said I'm a suspected escort. You can't really argue with them because you're trapped." Commenting on the case, Jon Davidson, legal director of Lambda Legal, complained: "Their agents need cultural awareness training to not misunderstand that people who simply are leading a normal sex life are not prostitutes." (Never mind people who are both leading a normal sex life and are prostitutes.) The stakes of context here are dire; a nude photo in a gallery is art, but in the wrong hands and on the wrong app is evidence of prostitution.

To distinguish art work from pornography, reviewers often insist on commenting on the disposition of the subject. Of Merritt's photo that transfixed him, on Page 66, David Bowman elaborated: "But it is the girl's expression that is a complete mystery. She's not posing as faked-up porno. She does not appear to be enjoying the particular penis she is sucking—not that she finds it distasteful." *Art in America* described Sepuya's *Darkroom Mirror (_2060403)* thus: "Sepuya photographs himself giving a joyless blowjob while a second dick waits in the wings." One does not appear to be enjoying; the other is joyless. There is an insistence against reading pleasure into what either artist is doing. Neither looks joyful, to my eye, but I wouldn't presume to know what their joy looks like. With a dick in one's mouth, how many legible expressions can one even make?

Legibility requires an audience; legible simply means decipherable, begging the question of what, exactly, it was that was deciphered. In art, as in sex work, legibility is often shrouded and unstable, constantly in question, emerging from a delicate scaffolding of intention, guesswork, clues, context. What is formally indistinguishable from porn, or dating app photos, or ad photos, is made legible as art because of where it is shown and who sees it and how pointedly they interpret it, and vice versa. Images are translated by their viewers and critics, to profound legal, social, and financial consequence: the art writer, the border patrol agent, the lonely traveler, the would-be buyer, the person on the other end of the phone.

~

In his famed 1972 performance art piece *Seedbed*, Vito Acconci masturbated while hidden underneath a foot-ramp in a SoHo gallery. Acconci's work was widely considered to be narcissistic, so much so that he later lamented, "Seedbed might have made my career, but it also destroyed it."

Acconci's own protocol describes the piece this way:

> Half-way across the room, the floor becomes a ramp that rises gradually to a height of two and a half feet at the far wall. Each day, the piece is open, from 10 A.M. to 6 P.M.: I'm underneath the ramp, moving under the viewers' floor—I'm masturbating, I keep my masturbation going by building sexual fantasies on the footsteps above me. The viewer enters the clean white space; the viewer hears a voice from below.

Photographs of the exhibit are strange: the room is barren, the walls white, with the floor sloping upward. Photographs of Acconci beneath the ramp are even stranger: the structure appears haphazard, with small supportive beams jutting between floor and ramp at odd angles, Acconci curled among them, jerking off in a fetal position. It looks claustrophobic. As visitors walked and sat above him, they heard his voice saying things like "I'm pressing my eyes into your hair." In a 1991 interview, Richard Prince asked Acconci, "Did you really ever have an orgasm under the Seedbed?" "Yes," he answered, and it's not hard to imagine how. His positioning is abject, humiliating—one of the great aphrodisiacs. But asked a similar question in 2007—"Could you find it sexy?"—he clarified, "It was more of a performance. It was like, this is my job, this is what I have to do."

Reviewing the piece in 1980, Germano Celant wrote, "All art is pornography if it assumes the right to impose on others personal pleasures and ideas. It is at this philosophic moment that Acconci removes himself from the scene and goes into exile; he intuits that the artist is an obscene exhibitionist who enjoys himself by entrapping others." Perhaps Acconci is equal opportunity with his entrapment: he traps the viewer into participating, but only after he ensnares himself, caught within an underground web of his own making. In her 1972 review of the work, April Kingsley asked, "How intimate or self-revelatory can art be, and still be art and not life?"

Asked by Prince what he found pornographic, Acconci answered, "A conversation in which a man keeps touching a woman's arm, a man on the street looking back at a woman who's just walked by; a man kissing goodbye a woman he's just met . . . and probably a woman doing the same. I don't know if these things are pornographic, but they're probably obscene." What Acconci describes as pornographic are largely boundary violations. Prince doesn't ask him if he considers his own work pornographic, but he does ask if he's ever wanted to create something "but thought, 'Even I couldn't get away with that?'" to which Acconci elides the *adult* entirely: "There have been pieces I didn't know how to do, so I never worked them out far enough to put out. In the early days, there was an idea of some performance on a floor filled with babies." Perverse; genius.

Last night, I dreamed that I performed a masturbation piece at MoMA. I was in a lobby of some kind, with a cot and a Hitachi magic wand. A gallerist organized the performance for me; it was as though we were renting a booth at a museum, as though museums were like barber shops, or commercial art fairs. A famous lesbian painter visited the installation and offered tacit approval. After everyone walked around, photographing and inspecting the set-up, I got in position to perform, half covering myself with a blanket. At some point the floors caved in and we all fell onto subway tracks filled with several feet of water as the museum's foundation gave way. Amid the rush of water, I approached my gallerist: "I don't know why I'm doing this performance for free," I told her. "What is the point? Can I charge people $100 if they want to watch me, and then take them to a private room? Even the bathroom would be fine." She mulled it over, said she'd ask the museum.

Once in a Midtown hotel, a client arranged me on the bed and directed me to masturbate for him. I felt a bit like a painting, albeit one in motion, but barely—the composition just so, only one appendage slowly moving. He stood off to the side, watching. I don't remember if he was touching himself or not; I was consumed by my own experience as a prop. A timer on his phone went off, signifying the end of the hour he'd paid for, and he abruptly began getting dressed to leave, with barely a word. I flipped over, pulling my stockings back on so as not to remain the only exposed party, now watching him. I felt I had failed at something. His sudden willingness to abandon our built world exactly at the moment previously delineated—so unlike most clients—seemed to indicate that I had failed to seduce him. Perhaps, though, he just needed to adhere to the boundary for his own reasons. Rules and walls are often what allow people to feel free to fully inhabit their desires; to direct another to touch themselves, or to otherwise demand precisely what they want. And artists need rules and walls, too. Though rules narrow the scope of what might happen, they are also a precursor to any action happening at all. A total lack of boundaries, on the other hand, often means creative paralysis.

In his 1969 work *Following Piece*, Acconci followed a different stranger every day, for one month, in New York City; the piece's only rule was that he followed until the person went into a private place he could not enter. Abiding by this rule allowed Acconci to fully embody his work; of it, he said, "I am almost not an 'I' anymore; I put myself in the service of this scheme."

In November 1974, Lynda Benglis's now-infamous dildo-adorned self-portrait was published in the advertising pages of *Artforum*. She paid double for the ad, to cover the possibility of the magazine incurring additional costs if their printer was aghast at the content. She ran the piece as an ad only when it was rejected as an art centerfold. She wears a massive double-ended dildo, hand on her hip, elbow jutted out, body glistening, spray tan lines visible, hair slicked back, sunglasses covering her gaze, which, I imagine, is pointed directly at the camera. Her nipples are bare; her rib cage is protruding. The image is more humorous than erotic, but it is also bold and arresting. Roberta Smith, co-chief art critic of the *New York Times*—and the first woman to hold the position—recalled, "It really was an amazing photograph. I remember the shock of seeing it and am always surprised at how shocking it remains. It is laugh-out-loud thrilling, and the phallus is the least of it."

My father brought up this image to me around my own artwork. I was telling him about my interpretation of the work of Andrea Fraser, whom he had never heard of, and he asked if I knew Benglis's. I said I did; I remembered reading a *New Inquiry* piece about the ad, written by a woman who taught an experimental sex education class I participated in a few years back. My dad brought it up as a kind of warning around my own public sexual experimentation, albeit kindly: "Women are often only remembered for that," he said. "It took years for her to be recognized primarily as a sculptor, after that."

While Benglis wasn't advertising a sexual service, her piece evokes sex ads, even more so by virtue of appearing in the advertising pages. Such analysis, though, is largely and curiously absent from critical reflections on the work, perhaps because her decision to publish it as an ad was not her original intention. Richard Meyer explains,

> According to Benglis, *Artforum* insisted that the name of a gallery appear somewhere in the ad so that readers would not think that the artist was advertising herself. With Cooper's permission, Benglis included [Paula Cooper's Gallery] but did so in "white [print], very very small, on black glossy ground, and the figure was on the other side of the page."

However, Benglis was not advertising an upcoming show, and paid for the placement herself.

Readers were scandalized; schools canceled their subscriptions; five out of six editors condemned Benglis's work in the following issue, and two subsequently resigned. In their December 1974 letter, the editors wrote, "For the first time in the 13 years of *Artforum*'s existence, a group of associate editors feel compelled to dissociate themselves publicly from a portion of the magazine's content, specifically the copyrighted advertisement of Lynda Benglis photographed by Arthur Gordon . . ." They went on to specify their belief that *Artforum* was committed to women's liberation, and that Benglis's ad "reads as a shabby mockery of the aims of that movement, *as well as* pictur[ing] the journal's role as devoted to the self-promotion of artists in the most debased sense of that term." The editors' disavowal of Benglis's work while being "aware of the economic interdependencies which govern the entire chain of artistic production and distribution" is plainly disingenuous. They simply disliked the mode in which Benglis chose to engage in self-promotion, which is ingenious, given the aforementioned economic interdependencies. Benglis herself described her work as a satire of "the art-star system, and the way artists use themselves, their persona, to sell the work."

What most viewers focus on in her ad is the dildo. Most analyses invariably describe it as "the phallus," attempting to elevate the toy several intellectual levels by using its Latin signifier, cloaked with heavy symbolism. Meyer laments, "Critics and curators tend to look through or past the image to find the message they want it to provide, whether it be that Benglis 'explicitly collapsed the phallus with the penis' . . . or 'subvert[ed] the psychic symbology of the penis itself.' The high-mindedness of such prose robs the image of its sexual lawlessness and graphic immediacy." But even Meyer is unable to categorize the ad as "either a feminist critique of pornography or a pornographic critique of feminism." I choose to see it as the latter.

At a time when second-wave feminists and radical lesbians were trying to organize a feminist movement against pornography around analyses like Robin Morgan's "pornography is the theory, and rape the practice," Benglis, too, was "really studying pornography," in her own words. Her studies resulted in an abrasive and wild self-portrait, gripping her own cock; theirs in the assertion that—from Andrea Dworkin, this time—"I don't want to be part of a movement that has a sense of priorities that says, 'Sticking a dildo up my vagina is more important than [fighting] pornography as an institution of sexual abuse for women.'" Further, such feminists often disavowed both dildos and women with dicks, believing any cock or cock-like object to be a violent tool of patriarchy; as Dworkin felt, "men use the penis to deliver death to women." (Unsurprisingly, these women were always anti-prostitution crusaders, as well.)

I read Benglis's ad less as a commentary on the psychosexual significance of the phallus and more as a visual representation of *girls just wanna have fun*. Her gender presentation is ambiguous; at the time, it would have been uncommon for critics to acknowledge the possibility that she was presenting her gender differently, as opposed to making a comment about gender. Forty years on, in 2014, Kathe Burkhart explored this idea: "She's performing gender, not performing 'male.' Phallic women who don't cleave to the 'norms' of a gender binary are still the elephant in the room. It's still a touchstone image for me, which existed before we had the term gender non-conforming." She holds her dick, extending from her body. She can do whatever she wants.

Not everyone so easily enjoys this aesthetic freedom, though. Also speaking in 2014, LaToya Ruby Frazier recalled the limits of the piece, saying it represents

> social and economic exclusivity and inequality. How many artists can afford to take out a $3,000 advertisement? How many non-white women artists are represented by galleries in New York City? . . . As an African-American woman from a working-class background, I am aware that my artistic labor and artwork are devalued when compared to male artists as well as white women artists.

At the moment of the ad, Benglis's artistic labor was valued and acknowledged—indeed, in the same issue, a reviewer painstakingly wrote about her sculpture work—affording her the opportunity, financially and otherwise, to question and play with that recognition, while daring her audience to see or interpret something else. As Frazier points out, for so many Black and working-class artists, such institutional recognition and financial compensation remain elusive in the first place.

Artist and filmmaker Tourmaline's first solo show took place in January 2021. Along with her world-renowned short film *Salacia*—which reimagines the life of Mary Jones, a Black trans sex worker who lived in 1800s New York City, and whose life's record was, before Tourmaline's intervention, all but lost to a few court records—she debuted five self-portraits, "drawing on Victorian-era pornography and turning it inside out," as Tiana Reid wrote in *4Columns*. Reid goes on, "the photographs of *Pleasure Garden*, taken together, emote possibility, construct a horizon of the limitlessness, disrupt received narratives about what black trans women are expected to endure. There are entire academic and artistic disciplines about how blackness and gender are co-constitutive (or co-disruptive). *Salacia* is in conversation with this rich dialogue about how blackness undermines normative articulations of gender." Tourmaline's self-portraiture is stunning and carefully evocative of, in her own words, "Black-owned pleasure gardens. Places where Black people, in this moment before 1827 when slavery was still legal in New York, would go and be able to be with each other in nature, and have some sociality with each other."

Unlike Benglis, Tourmaline interrogates a social positioning in which Black trans women have frequently been denied recognition of their womanhood, pushed to conform to cis standards of femininity so as to be easily legible to dominant culture, and disproportionately subjected to gendered interpersonal and state violence. In March 2021, New York finally repealed what had colloquially become known as the "walking while trans" law; ostensibly a tool to fight prostitution, the law gave cops wide latitude to arrest anyone they perceived to be "loitering with intent to commit prostitution." This empowered police to target, in particular, trans women of color, whom they presume, usually incorrectly, to be selling sex. Arrested under the statute in 2018 when she was just talking to her friends, a twenty-three-year-old trans woman from the Bronx—given the pseudonym "Raquel" for privacy—explained to *The Cut*, "People always think of a trans woman: 'You have to sell sex. That's your dominant job.' And that's not what everybody does." In a conversation published by *Document Journal*, with friends and fellow musicians Juliana Huxtable and Nomi Ruiz, on the joys and meaning of the underground club scene, and the kinds of work available to trans women in New York, DJ Honey Dijon explains,

> [During] my formative years in New York, nightlife, clubs, and music were safe havens for the creative community. Not just trans people, but a lot of different types of artists, and a lot of different types of gender expression . . . There were a lot of different ways to make your money without doing sex work or dealing drugs. That's why I'm so vocal about it: Club culture, for me, is not just entertainment.

Still, the profiling by law enforcement persists. Of the "walking while trans" statute, Melissa Gira Grant writes, "Sex workers and anyone perceived to be a sex worker are believed to always be working, or, in the cops' view, always committing a crime." The material and social outcomes of such fabricated perception are severe.

Of *Pleasure Garden*, Tourmaline told *Artforum*,

> Part of this exhibition has been the experience of me going to Chapter Gallery's pop-up location on Madison Street, which is literally just three blocks away from the mutual aid society that started Seneca Village and this place owned by the Lyons family that was a refuge for Black sailors. And I'm there, watching people look at this exposed version of me . . .

Tourmaline watches people watch her; watches people take in what are, in fact, exquisite nudes—museum-quality-nudes—and accept or shy away from the pleasure she offers them. She is in control of her image, inviting her own visibility and voyeurism. The art world strives to de-sexualize even its most erotic works; people take such pains to view sexually evocative art seriously and sterile-ly, as though it were impossible for sex to be both hot and serious, for art to be both weighty and wet. Tourmaline's work is astonishing precisely because it is an invitation to fall softly into the messy erotics of it all; warm and inviting, her images are a party, not a doctor's appointment. Further, she attacks the glass ceiling of a market oversaturated with nudes; by shifting their context, hers go for tens of thousands of dollars a pop.

In preparation for the show, Tourmaline's gallery sent her a first draft of image descriptions for her self-portraits. In *Swallowtail*, she reclines in dry grass, corset pulled down and skirt pulled up, pearls caught in her teeth. Her legs are open, and her dick rests between them, peeking out from beneath the white fabric of her gown. I sat with her as she looked over them, visiting her high-rise studio to chat about nothing and look at the city, as I often do. The image description for *Swallowtail* referenced a visible "phallus"; "I don't know if I want to use that word," she said. I asked what she wanted to use, and she said, "What sounds the most fun?" Tourmaline is disinterested in both respectability and—its relative—the discursive sanitizing of the body; I believe she and Benglis have this in common. After all, Benglis says, "I think artists create their own rules—or break them."

Tourmaline's Wikipedia page still identifies her as an "activist," in spite of her photographs and films sitting in the permanent collections of every major museum in New York City, and others worldwide. The creative and intellectual work of Black people, particularly if it draws on their relationships to their own identities, is often heralded as activism, rather than art or scholarship. In August 2020, writer and researcher Dr. Zoé Samudzi tweeted, "I can't wait till I'm invited to talk about white supremacy-related stuff and people stop calling me an 'activist.' I'm literally a sociologist *studying* genocide and white nationalism lmao . . . it's just very apparent the different ways people don't fully acknowledge or take seriously your work even as they're inviting you to speak on something." Aruna D'Souza, art critic and curator, replied: "People do this to me all the time and it's embarrassing because I haven't actually done the work to be considered an activist. But apparently there's no way to be understood as an art critic or a writer if you're not stanning for whiteness, so activist is the best they can do?"

To be clear, Tourmaline was an activist for many years; she worked as a community organizer for more than a decade and, in that time, uncovered archival footage and ephemera on Marsha P. Johnson, Sylvia Rivera, and their grassroots coalition STAR (Street Transvestite Action Revolutionaries), whose outreach and housing provisions for young, homeless trans people was funded through whoring and hustling. She single-handedly made this archive public and accessible. But this is not her work anymore.

Who the canon recognizes as an artist, and who (when their identity is in vogue) is celebrated as an activist for their art is telling. Johnson was both a sex worker and a visionary performance artist; she performed internationally with the drag troupe Hot Peaches, as well as putting on surreal and jubilant shows on street corners in the Village. And further, she walked down Christopher Street naked—for which she was arrested, jailed, and forcibly medicated, treated as mentally ill—while Madonna hitchhiked naked in Miami a few decades on, photographed by Steven Meisel, and was heralded as a transgressive pop icon.

For trans people, the question of legibility is not just about earning potential and proper recognition of their work, but rife with physical violence as well: when the police are incited against trans women and sex workers; when trans women are barred from safely accessing public spaces (like restrooms) in which they are less likely to suffer harassment or violence. As most clearly stated by TERFS and SWERFs—trans-exclusionary and sex work–exclusionary radical feminists—these violent forms of coercion and surveillance are based on the belief that trans women and sex workers are not real women and, thus, deserve violence. Gira Grant puts it succinctly: "We permit some violence against women to be committed in order to protect the social and sexual value of other women." Such commitment to a particular brand of feminism—the kind that blanket-decries pornographic images of women's bodies in magazines, in galleries, and on the internet; the kind that brandishes womanhood as a club for which only the right kind of suffering guarantees entry—is cruel, destructive, and narrow. It is tragic, and it is also boring. A movement obsessed by the legitimacy of its own suffering and the illegitimacy of the suffering of others is asphyxiated from the start. It is the duty of everyone to recognize that the desperate shouts against inclusion and autonomy for all are coming from an animated corpse and to dismiss them accordingly.

And this is the great gift that Tourmaline and Benglis give us: work that is oxygenated, alive, and released of binding strictures. Tourmaline's favorite saying is "Nothing serious is going on here"; Benglis, now an octogenarian, reflects, "I put some humour into the women's movement. It was needed." It is the daring and brilliant girls who go the deepest and the slipperiest, reveling in the unrestrained play of their work, knowing the last laugh will always be theirs.

On Meaning, Part II

Leonard Cohen writes,

> Because you are close,
> everything that men make, observe
> or plant is close, is mine.

Samuel Delany writes,

> Desire and knowledge (body and mind) are not a fundamental opposition; rather, they are intricately imbricated and mutually constitutive aspects of political and social life. Situations of desire . . . are the first objects and impellers of intellectual inquiry . . . [and] we might give more thought to the necessary and productive aspect of this imbrication of knowledge and desire as it expresses itself so positively in so many forms of contact, before—with a wrecking ball and even more sweeping legislation—we render [the] central structure asexual and "safe" in the name of family values and corporate giantism.

Adrienne Rich writes,

> *What does love mean*
> *what does it mean "to survive"*
> *A cable of blue fire ropes our bodies*

burning together in the snow We will not live
to settle for less We have dreamed of this
all of our lives.

Larry Mitchell writes,

> The strong women told the faggots that there are two important things to remember about the coming revolutions. The first is that we will get our asses kicked. The second is that we will win. The faggots knew the first. Faggot ass-kicking is a time-honored sport of the men. But the faggots did not know about the second. They had never thought about winning before. They did not even know what winning meant. So they asked the strong women and the strong women said winning was like surviving, only better.

M. E. O'Brien writes,

> When refusing their imposed disposability and isolation through revolutionary activity, junkies and their friends move towards a communism not based on the dignity of work, but on the unconditional value of our lives.

Muriel Rukeyser writes,

> The potflower on the windowsill says to me
> In words that are green-edged red leaves :
> Flower flower flower flower
> Today for the sake of all the dead Burst into flower.

I text my boyfriend from the other room, "Am I a worker?" I am reading Marxist theory, and I am confused. I don't understand whether or not I own my own means of production; I'm not sure what it means when you use your own labor power to sell a commodity if that commodity is, in the end, your self. The Clandestine Whores Network, "an expanded collective of sex workers against work," write in their futurist-utopian manifesto, "We have no illusions of what is at stake, and we have the clarity that our criminal potential escalates with the formation of bonds with other criminals—with gangs, widows, drifters, homeless youth, scammers, users, those passing through to other borders, and those who we will say we never saw." When I read theory, I get turned around; when I read this, I remember. I align myself with the criminals, not just the workers. Professionalism is the enemy of us all.

This manifesto—"Beneath Everything"—describes a utopian future accessible only through communal criminality. I read it when it was first published in 2019 by *Pinko*—a magazine publisher and collective whose tagline is "Communism for fags!"—and it felt like discovering I could breathe underwater. I had stumbled upon a future I wanted, something that both reflected myself back to me and directed my gaze outward toward things that felt at the same time entirely new and tenderly familiar. Rejection of the state and its counterparts—cops, prisons, snitches, the professional-managerial class—is implicit in the Network's adamant embrace of all those who exist on the outskirts of capitalist discipline. They introduce themselves:

> We are whores who draw power from our particular criminal tendency. To be clandestine; illicit, secret, hidden. Historically, a clandestine prostitute was one who refused to work within the confines of the law, or limited how her body was subjugated by it. Embracing the clandestine is to

nurture resistance and more expansive forms of solidarity with people in the criminal underclass today. It is on this principle that the following future begins.

Clandestine prostitutes refused to register with vice police—a registration that would legally label them in such a way that was, often, simply inaccurate: they didn't necessarily identify with prostitution as their profession or even main source of income. Clandestine prostitution speaks to a wider array of people who trade sex for money or other survival needs, whether regularly, occasionally, or sporadically, in a pinch. There is a common phrase that gets shared around on social media, printed on buttons, put on T-shirts for things like International Whores' Day, or International Day to End Violence Against Sex Workers: "Someone I love is a sex worker." But I've also seen it changed to the more aggressive, and potent: "Someone *you* love is a sex worker." If you think you don't know anyone who has ever sold sex, you are almost certainly mistaken.

The Network writes the world they want into existence, describing a future seven years on that glows with generative autonomy and camaraderie. They describe modes of techno-resistance—"We know the entire network of surveillance cameras in each hotel, each street corner, every bar, and have a consistent method of mapping and tracking which have been destroyed"—and tactics friends use to keep one another as safe and free as possible from sexual violence—"when you're not able to escape, there's a panic button underneath the headboard, alerting others in your in-call space to act immediately . . . For incidents that cannot be solved by personal interference, snipers are stationed at strategic points, especially for out-call appointments with new clients, when we are at our most vulnerable"—rendering police irrelevant, obsolete. This collective caretaking and cultivating of revolutionary potential fosters conditions necessary for rest, time off, art-making:

> There are so many creative projects by whores, a whole wave of new cinema by black prostitutes, autonomous hoe anthologies, sex worker science fiction novels, we don't even know of all of them. We encounter them on the bed-sides of new lovers, or in the spare bedroom of a comrade who lets us crash while we work for a bit in their city.

Theirs is a world where boundaries are intentionally porous, slipping through borders goes unnoticed, and confusing algorithms and defying legibility is encouraged.

I would guess that the Network demands a militant commitment to mutual aid and a militant code against narcing, but beyond that, who, exactly, one wants to be, and how, exactly, they want to identify, seem entirely up to the individual. Their manifesto assures, "Sabbaticals are openly encouraged. Quitting the work for other pursuits is natural and never leads to expulsion or displacement." Identity is less important than critical thought or critical commitment. The Network's vision stands, to me, in stark opposition to visions put forth by other factions of the sex workers' rights movement and regurgitated in mainstream news outlets reporting on the normalization of sex work. They speak of whoring as a mode through which other aspects of life are made more livable; indeed, most vice crime functions as a means to that same end. Whoring, gambling, drinking, drugging—each seeks to shift material or affective conditions to make life a little easier, a little better, a little faster, a little slower. Professionalized work functions as a mode of social discipline, producing the rote and the assimilable; de-professionalized whoring functions as a mode of social chaos, allowing for cracks and hacks within and around the idea that one must work, formally, in order to deserve to live.

I like, at this point, how little anyone around me associates me with having a job. I don't have a job. There's the now-famous aphorism, shared so often that its attribution is lost: Someone asks, "What's your dream job?" and someone answers, "I do not dream of labor." What to dream of, then? I dream of strange sky-worlds; the dirty ocean at Rockaway Beach; the ecstatic feeling in the middle of a second glass of wine; the juvenile romance of blood oaths; seeing again those I grew up with who have since died, on some other translucent plane; the perfect sliced mango that I ate once with my closest friend, a conduit to God in an unassuming plastic container; a place where it is never winter and I am never sad. Of cops swallowed by a wave. Of prison bars spontaneously turning to dust. Of welding an enormous metal sculpture that says all of the things I would like it to say without using any words. Of staying in bed all day. Of everyone doing exactly as they want. Of my favorite hoof shoes in a color that does not yet exist. Of new sex with new people that is complicated but faultless. Of my orange cat living to thirty. Of marrying my boyfriend. Of having babies. Of playing with other people's babies. Of a performance in which the floor is full of babies, like Acconci wanted.

moses moon writes,

> what do we actually *mean* when we say "sex work is work"? Are we attempting to normalize it? Are we aligning it with other types of work? Do we want to legalize it so that it is like other labor? Why do we pay taxes? Are

> we making a case for inclusivity? . . . My major question is: Can we move beyond "sex work is work"? Perhaps to engaging the phrase "sex work is (anti)work"? Past normalization?

I hold ardent solidarity with all who commit crimes and all who have dreams. I seek affinity with those who want to work as little as possible; with those who can't work. My boyfriend used to wear a leather jacket with these words painted on: *IF WE ALL SPIT AT ONCE THEY WILL DROWN*. It was a bastardization of a quote from Bob Crow, RMT Union general secretary, in England: "If we all spit together we can drown the bastards." It's a delicious image, deluging those who want us unorganized, underpaid, exploited—with our own saliva.

I sleep over at the house of a guy who I've known for years; he has just changed jobs. He went from working for a boss to working for himself; I ask if he still has to work every day. "Yes," he rolls his eyes, "I still have to work every day." Then, teasing: "I forgot, lucky you, you don't work." Whereas once I would have been offended, now I'm thrilled; you couldn't give me a better compliment. "I sure don't," I answer. Momentarily defensive: "But I pay my rent!" Another eye roll: "I know." I smile, and go back to sleep.

A fantasy persists that capitalism is not a totalizing system of domination. A fantasy persists that spheres of our private lives are able to function outside of capital's grasp; that it is possible to keep sacred, emotional, creative, and interpersonal spaces apart from capital's hold over the rest of our lives. Part of the fantasy is that preserving these spaces apart is, in fact, desirable and possibly even transgressive against capital. This is untrue.

Tiqqun writes that for those who have capitulated to Empire's permanent grasp,

> [existence] is now nothing but a lifelong struggle to render oneself compatible with Empire. But for the others, for us, every gesture, every desire, every affect encounters, at some distance, the need to annihilate Empire . . . Following this criminal path, we have the time; nothing obliges us to seek out direct confrontation . . . Retaking the offensive for our side is a matter of making the battlefield manifest. The figure of the Young-Girl is a *vision machine* conceived to this effect.

The anarchist prostitute, the artist whoring herself out, and the whore spending nearly every waking hour on her art—she takes on the call of the vision machine; she strives to make the battlefield manifest. She loathes Empire with all her big, beautiful, calculating heart, and yet she knows everything she does, makes, loves, fucks, and kills is born and dies within it. Admitting that what we hold dear is not outside of the grasp of the system we revile is not admitting defeat; it is accurately assessing the conditions so that we might fight back. Like Marlo says in the famous scene from *The Wire*, when he—ruthless and all-powerful head of the city's largest drug operation—steals candy while staring into the face of the corner store's security guard, purely to show he can do whatever he wants, and is then confronted by the security guard outside, who protests, "I am a man, I'm here"—like Marlo says, then, sucking on the lollipop he stole: "You want it to be one way—but it's the other way." The power of Empire functions *the other way.*

Foucault explains power as insidious and disciplining, composed of myriad "relations," as opposed to one discrete and brutal force. In his first volume of *The History of Sexuality*, he advances these propositions:

> Relations of power are not in a position of exteriority with respect to other types of relationships (economic processes, knowledge relationships, sexual relations), but are immanent in the latter; they are the immediate effects of the divisions, inequalities, and disequilibriums which occur in the latter, and conversely they are the internal conditions of these differentiations; relations of power are not in superstructural positions, with merely a role of prohibition or accompaniment; they have a directly productive role, wherever they come into play . . . Power comes from below; that is, there is no binary and all-encompassing opposition between rulers and ruled at the root of power relations.

For Foucault, power is not merely a thing exercised *over* us, *by* rulers, or institutions; it is not wielded, held, or lost. It is produced within and around any relation, produced and reproduced by our participation in normative institutions and, just as often, by our resistance to normative institutions. Thus, attempts to demarcate our lives into categories within and outside of commodification—commonly called the *work-life balance*—are more than futile: such attempts actively reinscribe the dominance of capitalist work as the defining structure of our lives.

To imagine that sex could or should be protected from commodification under our current economic system is to deny the diffuse nature of the imagined boundary between work and life, and to resign ourselves to a paltry vision of what our interpersonal relationships to and around sex can be. And when I say sex, I mean *our sex lives*, not sex as a tool for marketing, not the sex in *sex sells*. Here is an example: if a person works 9 to 5 in an office, they are likely not having sex on the clock. They get home at six; their partner, who has a longer commute, gets home at seven thirty. One of them showers; the other orders takeout. They are tired, and they check their emails. One of them takes a phone call from a colleague working remotely in a time zone three hours earlier.

They have left work but they are still preoccupied by it, even though they are now in life's territory. They binge-watch a television show, which probably makes a joke at the expense of sex workers; most of my favorite shows do. This is not a commentary on whether or not the modern, working couple is having good sex, or having sex frequently, or even on whether or not they are having the kind of sex they want to have—it is merely a statement of fact, that whatever sex they are having is structured, at every turn, by the limitations of their working lives, because their working lives structure both survival (and its obstacles) and leisure: schedule, sleep, income, health insurance, disability, geographic location, energy. And as work from home becomes more common, the boundary between work life and domestic life, work life and erotic life, breaks down even further, casting a shadow of unproductivity and guilt on all non-work activity done at home, particularly during traditional working hours.

Money and survival dominate so much of our psychic life under capitalism. I have seen a dear friend through a psychotic break; at its apex, he lucidly panicked about income lost to his present circumstances of in-and-out catatonia. He stayed at our place that week, and I had work scheduled on his worst day. He sat in the bathtub with the shower on while my boyfriend got ready to take him to the hospital and while I debated canceling. I wouldn't be allowed into the hospital though—Covid restrictions—and so I shaved my legs in our kitchen sink while our friend suffered under a stream of water, went to the appointment, turned my brain off, and called my boyfriend as soon as I got out. They were still waiting in the psych ER, hours on.

There is no outside to work, if work in this reading is a metonym for the material and psychic circumstances of those who must earn a wage to trade for the basic rights of housing, food, medical care, child care, pleasures, and autonomy. And, indeed, in a Foucaultian way, maintaining that there is an outside to work only produces a power relation that reinforces the disciplining apparatuses of work; the couple, or the family, or the friends, participate in a mutual make-believe wherein they are truly off when they are off, as opposed to off in relation to work, off inflected by work. The illusion of off-time and its benefits facilitates their acquiescence to on-time; "at least we get a weekend," they might say, "at least we have this vacation." The greatest relief freedom from a daily job gives me is not having to dread work—not the individual act of working, but the endless concept, extending forever out in front, always upcoming and overtaking—as opposed to a discrete event bracketed by whatever else I want to do.

Nonetheless, my perspective is not the dominant one. Myriad self-help gurus, books, and articles extoll the foundational importance of achieving work-life balance and offer tricks to do just so—"37 Tips for a Better Work-Life Balance"; "Post Covid, What Work-Life Balance Needs"; "4 Easy Ways to Maintain a Healthy Work-Life Balance"; "Creating Work-Life Balance When Returning to Office"—squarely pitting work and life against one another. This creates what is both a necessary and misleading dichotomy. The dichotomy is misleading for the reasons previously outlined; the dichotomy is also necessary because one assumes that without it, life would simply be subsumed within work—life, the wave, and work, the ocean. Tellingly, for example, Jeff Bezos is an opponent of the work-life balance concept and instead pushes for "work-life harmony." In a 2018 interview with Mathias Döpfner, CEO of *Business Insider*'s parent company, Bezos proclaimed the virtues of integrating life and work:

> This work-life harmony thing is what I try to teach young employees and actually senior executives at Amazon too. But especially the people coming in. I get asked about work-life balance all the time. And my view is, that's a debilitating phrase because it implies there's a strict trade-off. And the reality is, if I am happy at home, I come into the office with tremendous energy. And if I am happy at work, I come home with tremendous energy. It actually is a circle; it's not a balance.

Meanwhile, Amazon warehouse workers face inhumane and untenable conditions: grueling hours, frequent injuries, constant surveillance, limited and monitored bathroom breaks, low wages, fierce anti-unionization tactics. In the words of a formerly incarcerated warehouse worker who subsequently quit: "I would rather go back to a state correctional facility and work for 18 cents an hour than do that job."

In her anti-work treatise *The Problem with Work*, Kathi Weeks writes, "I want to consider *life* as a possible counterpoint to work . . . I want to explore the political project of *life against work* as a general rubric within which to frame the kinds of antiwork critiques and postwork imaginaries represented here by the demands for basic income and shorter hours." She acknowledges the risks of such a demarcation being "recuperated into the logic of commodity culture," but nonetheless offers life against work not as a static concept but as a liberationist gesture "to be continually invented in the struggle to mark distinctions between fields of experience that nonetheless remain intertwined." I read her call for distinction as a hopeful attempt, acknowledging its inherent failure as a clean-cut or linear project, and in so doing, morphing and spawning and evading cooptation by arms of capital. Illegibility might provide us protection, and room to discover.

As a safeguard against the failures implicit in "life against work," Weeks dissects and ultimately champions the colloquial phrase "get a life," arguing for it as a profound intervention in modern work culture. She details its capacity as a revolutionary phrase, its implication that there will be a multitude of lives still to get, and the getting of those lives as a necessarily collective project—*a* life, one among many. She explains, "Though it is a life that would be ours, as a life rather than a commodity, as a web of relations and qualities of experience rather than a possession, it is not something we can be said precisely to own or even to hold." And that is where pockets free from capital lie, where meaning itself lies: in the *ours* that we neither possess, nor regulate, nor fully understand, but encounter and float within and steal, like a bioluminescent sea, or a CitiBike we joyride in the woods upstate, grown mossy and rusty from laying, rogue, in a creek. Incidentally, such an *ours* is often found through art or sex.

I saw an image online, a drawing of a fantastical and hermaphroditic girl-child with their hair in pigtails tied with red ribbons at the ends, strange antlers or devil horns spanning outward from their head, naked, holding an enormous orange flower. A word bubble extends from their mouth, written in what looks like pencil: "Goodness didn't you kids ever see a flower this big?" I fell in love with the drawing. I discovered it was by outsider artist Henry Darger. *Of course.* This drawing encapsulated *ours* for me: an *ours* that I did not own but that expanded far beyond my grasp; that flowed from looking at the right place at the right time; that I was primed to love because my grandmother had loved Darger's work and taken me to a show of his drawings of which I remember only the colors and the eerie feeling; that evoked youthful innocence and destruction in equal measure; whose subject looked like me as a child, and how I appear sometimes now, in an approximation of myself as a child, with my Lolita style; that offered the magic of a huge flower, and of showing that flower—impossibly big and impossibly beautiful—to those you're playing with. All of these things made it *ours*. When my boyfriend fucks me in our bed while the sun streams through our window, chokes me—that's a vision of a sun-choked *ours*, of getting choked in the sun. These are the *qualities of experience* that make a life worth living: the art of the big flower; the erotics of the sunlight tickling the face of your beloved.

This *ours* is akin to José Esteban Muñoz's queer utopian futurity in *Cruising Utopia*, in which he argues that "queerness is not quite here; it is . . . a potentiality." The *ours*, the moments free of capitalism, are potentialities. Muñoz's use of hope is inherently anti-capitalist; he implores us to "dream and enact new and better pleasures, other ways of being in the world, and ultimately new worlds." These things that happen, that coalesce, that we see or make or do that feel use-less and good; that are neither constructive nor destructive but something else entirely—a moving of worlds wholly unrelated to a reality before or after.

Muñoz analyzes Frank O'Hara's famous love poem "Having a Coke with You," which goes on from the title,

> is even more fun than going to San Sebastian, Irún,
> Hendaye, Biarritz, Bayonne
> . . .

I look
at you and I would rather look at you than all
the portraits in the world
except possibly for the Polish Rider occasionally and
anyway it's in the Frick
which thank heavens you haven't gone to yet so we can go
together for the first time
and the fact that you move so beautifully more or less
takes care of Futurism.

Muñoz offers:

> The fun of having a Coke is a mode of exhilaration in which one views a restructured sociality. The poem tells us that mere beauty is insufficient for the aesthete speaker . . . If art's limit were beauty . . . it is simply not enough. The utopian function is enacted by a certain surplus in the work that promises a futurity, something that is not quite here . . . The anticipatory illumination of certain objects is a kind of potentiality that is open, indeterminate, like the affective contours of hope itself.

I went with my boyfriend to the Venice Biennale. I drank a lot of Cokes, which I like to do while I'm away from home. I attempted to reference this poem but he thought I was referencing the famous Coke commercial, and he said, "Which polar bear are you?" and I couldn't stop laughing. We went to the Frari to see Titian's *Assumption of the Virgin,* and I was hard-pressed to say which was more beautiful, the sixteenth-century altarpiece of Mary surrounded by angels or him, in his Carhartt pants and Warzone hoodie, long hair alight with the sun and surrounded by ancient marble. Watching him move about the church held the "affective contours of hope itself": Southern boy with his leather Harley-Davidson cap in his hands, telling me which pieces he thought were *sick*, us surrounded by water in a city so obscenely beautiful it seemed almost certainly fake.

In Venice, we ran into my mentor, and we spent her last night in the city getting drunk in the rain. One bar closed, and she led us to a different one she'd developed a fondness for on the trip, and they were out of the liquor we had been drinking so we all switched liquors and kept drinking. We parted late and I texted her photos I'd taken of the two of them walking in the downpour, writing "love you so much," and she sent back a zoomed-in photo of me, eyes squeezed shut to protect from the rain, smile squishing my face, bangs soaked on my forehead, looking like a child about to scream from excitement, "You too."

A state is altered; a hand held; a song heard; a baby swaddled; a photograph developed; a kiss, rushed and perfect, in a dark corner lit by the feeling of new futures unfolding, suddenly. These potentialities are different from a momentary feeling that all is right in the world; they are moments where this world has vanished entirely. I don't know how one could seek *a life* without the hope of a new world; I don't know how one could be satisfied with this one. There is so much more to feel, and to be had.

Here is another way to say all of this: as I prepared for a show in March 2021, I knew I wanted to develop a performance piece that involved having my blood drawn. I liked the idea of having my boyfriend draw my blood—both because I trust him with my life, and because I hoped to disrupt the easy feminist read of what I was doing. It's hard to use blood in performance art, as a woman, without it being read in a very particular lineage around either fertility or self-harm—but I wanted to use my blood mafia-style. Joseph Valachi, a member of the Genovese crime family turned informant—famous for being the first snitch to admit the existence of the Italian American mafia—broke omertà to describe his initiation ritual:

> I sit down at the table. There is wine. Someone put a gun and a knife in front of me. The gun was a .38 and the knife was what we call a dagger. Maranzano motions us up and we say some words in Italian. Then Joe Bonanno pricks my finger with a pin and squeezes until the blood comes out. What then happens, Mr. Maranzano says, "This blood means that we are now one Family. You live by the gun and the knife and you die by the gun and the knife."

If my punk boyfriend bloodlet me with sterile medical equipment, I reasoned, it might allow the blood to indicate contract and revenge, as opposed to if I cut myself, for example. But first, we had to learn how.

I texted my friend who is an anarchist nurse and happens to look a lot like Bettie Page, if Bettie Page were covered in tattoos. I asked if I could hire her to help us:

> I dont know if its possible to draw blood like that in a non-medical setting (like, is it possible to get the supplies and is it safe to do? I was reading about getting air bubbles in your blood and obv I dont wanna die [heart eyes emoji]) and idk if you know how to draw blood but I would imagine you do? So if it IS possible and possible to do safely and you know how, I would love to hire you to teach us how/get us the supplies? I know this is a super random/strange request lmao.

She responded immediately, "Hey! I can def teach him how to draw that way," and a few weeks later she came over to do so.

She stole the supplies from her job; she also brought us expired Narcan, which hospitals can't give out but harm reduction outreach projects, like my boyfriend's, can. This is the context through which I had met her—a friend hired her to do an overdose prevention training at their art show, and I subsequently hired her to do one at a show of mine. At that time, she was still in nursing school; she also worked for Planned Parenthood, and more than once gave me advice on gynecological healthcare, when I had bad insurance and wanted to avoid unnecessary doctor's appointments. She is very brilliant and very generous.

We sat in my living room as she explained what she'd brought—the kind of needle, the vials with anticoagulant, the latex gloves and the gauze. She explained to my boyfriend how to find a vein—that one should go by feel, rather than only sight. He tried and missed my vein, and then he tried again and bright red blood shot down through the tube attached to the needle and into the vial, flowing steadily. All the while, our other friend watched—the same friend who had months before suffered the psychotic break—drawing my name on napkins over and over, perfecting it in advance of tattooing it on my boyfriend's neck for our anniversary. I profusely thanked our teacher, and though she insisted I didn't have to pay her—that she loved teaching people skills with supplies she'd pilfered, that everyone should learn how to draw blood, and that in fact this was how she herself had learned, from a friend, because she wasn't taught properly in school—I was flush with cash from a newly lucrative work arrangement, and gave her a green envelope with five hundred-dollar bills inside. After they both left, I admired the scene on my red coffee table: a red sharps container, a dark red vial of blood, *Sophia* scripted onto napkins in curling letters.

I continued planning the performance. I booked the penthouse suite at the Bowery Hotel, paying the $3,000 plus tax out of pocket when my fledgling gallery couldn't afford the cost. I hired another friend to perform with me; she braided my hair at the beginning, before I read a piece on labor, extortion, failure, and revenge, and before my blood was drawn. She is a dancer, and her mother was visiting, and the two of them arrived together to the suite hours early to rehearse and helped me decide how to move the furniture around. Her mom sipped a Manhattan and wore her hair down at the request of her daughter. I didn't know either of them well but felt close and comfortable because the only other time I'd spent with them both together was my dancer friend's birthday camping trip, nearly a year earlier. She had maybe twenty friends on an island in the middle of the Hudson River, including her mom, whom she'd set up in an extra-large tent with a mattress inside. We tied floating tubes to trees on the island, letting them extend thirty, fifty yards out into the river, floating in the beating August sun. My boyfriend and I had sweaty sex in our tent and wolfed down the bread and hot-smoked salmon we'd brought as a snack, getting fish oil on the tent's nylon. I unilaterally hated camping before the trip; afterward, I decided I liked it, but only under particular and magical circumstances.

My point is, I knew everyone from pockets-out-of-Empire-time. I knew everyone from *ours* times—from giving out stolen medical supplies to people who need them on the street; from taking care of each other when our heads were sick; from being in love; from getting sunburned in freshwater while drinking beer from a sweaty can; from bringing different generations of people into the same party; from people saying *yes* to participating in a peculiar and at times unformed vision, allowing it to unfold in its own way, in its own time. And I could pay everyone well; and I could pay for the space; and I could pay for the photographer I hired to stay in his own suite in the same hotel, because it was his birthday in the morning; and I could have the martinis and wine I wanted as the opening party's drinks, and pay the bartender, and throw money at the last-minute problems that arose throughout the day, including a hotel staff member hushing us but relenting when we tipped generously, allowing us to midnight. I could pay for all of this because I was fucking for my money, and I had time to develop all of this because I was fucking for my money, and I met a lot of these people, and formed collaborative and strange relationships with them, because I was fucking for my money.

I don't know what this means other than that it felt prefigurative and that it was made possible through whoring. I made a pocket of a life that was lush and fair, a pocket of how I wish my world always was.

In "Revolutionary Letter No. 19," Diane di Prima writes,

> if what you want is jobs
> for everyone, you are still the enemy,
> you have not thought thru, clearly
> what that means

and then, in the final stanza,

> you are selling yourself short, remember
> you can have what you ask for, ask for
> everything.

But what is already *ours*, we need not ask for; through the cracks, we seize it.

I don't want to be a whore forever. I do want to be an artist forever. I hope we don't always have to work or sell to live.

When you first learn how to draw from life, through still life or figurative sketching, you are told one rule alone: *Draw what you see, not what you think you see*. Draw this apple, or this body, or this vase, as you really see it—not as an approximation of what you've been taught an apple, or a body, or a vase looks like.

I don't want to live an approximation of a life I've been taught to see, a life that I only think I see. I want to live a life that I see.

Acknowledgments

Thank you to:

Jessie Kindig, for believing in me and this book when everyone was inside and the future seemed like it would never come—and for your kindness, insight, and deep generosity every step of the way. Your impeccable shepherding has been a gift.

My dad, for being an artist; my mom, for being my mother—and for everything both of you have taught me, accepted, and loved. Julia Giovannitti, for taking care of me; I tried to say it other ways, but no words are enough. Nina Wineburgh, for your constancy and openness, and for staying with me as we grew. Sarah Chalfie and Molly Rappaport, for everything we've ever talked about, everything you've saved me from, and everything you've compelled me toward. Dave and Nard Justice—for softness and home, and all the rest, forever. Ripley Soprano, for being the first person to write with me, for your eternal friendship, and for thinking through together all the things we were taught not to think about. Charlotte Shane, for making me want to write before I ever met you. Tourmaline, for being the first and brightest flower to light the path, for our laughter and magic, and for teaching me to be all of myself. An Duplan, for seeing me as an artist. Sarah Michelson, for talking to me about art, the body, and womanhood like no one I'd ever met before. Mara McKevitt, for all the unknowns we stepped into together, holding hands. Syd Prescott, for always sharing what you know with joy. Sydney Fishman and Eden Deering, for nurturing my work and taking so many leaps of faith.

There are so many more people I've loved, read, heard, talked to, worked alongside, admired, and learned from, who have traces here.

Permissions Acknowledgments

"Nothing's Gonna Hurt You Baby"
Written by Gregory Steven Gonzalez
Copyright © 2012 Sleepy Bow Publishing
All Rights Administered Worldwide by Kobalt Music Publishing Ltd
All Rights Reserved Used by Permission
Reprinted by Permission of Hal Leonard LLC

Excerpt from "Other Writers," currently collected in *The Book of Longing*, copyright © 2006 by Leonard Cohen, used by permission of The Wylie Agency LLC and HarperCollins Publishers, reprinted by permission of Penguin Books Limited.

Excerpt from "Owning Everything," currently collected in *The Spice Box of Earth*, copyright © Leonard Cohen, 1961, used by permission of The Wylie Agency LLC.

The lines from "Phantasia for Elvira Shatayev," from *The Dream of a Common Language: Poems 1974–1977* by Adrienne Rich. Copyright © 1978 by W. W. Norton & Company, Inc. Used by permission of W. W. Norton & Company, Inc.

"The Power of Suicide"
Copyright © 2005 by Muriel Rukeyser
Reprinted by permission of ICM Partners

Notes

On Meaning, Part I

7 **sense & sex are boundless:** Diane di Prima, *Revolutionary Letters* (City Lights Books, 2021), 58.

On Fantasy

12 **My ambition is to be unmanageable:** H. C. Wilentz, "The Challenge of 'L'Inceste' and 'The Incest Diary,'" *New Yorker*, February 15, 2018, newyorker.com.

12 **the prostitute imaginary:** Melissa Gira Grant, *Playing the Whore: The Work of Sex Work* (Verso, 2014), 4.

13 **The world of the Young-Girl evinces:** Tiqqun, *Preliminary Materials for a Theory of the Young-Girl*, trans. Ariana Reines (Semiotext(e), 2012), 76.

13 **one of the last surviving Surrealists:** Elaine Mayers Salkaln, "The Mystery Woman," *New York Times*, October 13, 2002, 46.

14 **Fantasy is the means by which:** Lauren Berlant, *Cruel Optimism* (Duke University Press, 2011), 2.

14 **bride of the wind:** Salkaln, "Mystery."

15 **Art or whatever I call art:** Sarah Nicole Prickett, "First Interview: Artforum's New Editor-in-Chief David Velasco," *SSENSE*, January 2018, ssense.com.

16 **The manipulation of affect is stock-in-trade:** Nicholas Ridout and Rebecca Schneider, "Precarity and Performance: An Introduction," *TDR/The Drama Review* 56, no. 4 (Winter 2012).

17 **Also like, what's driving sex work:** Anh Vo, "Sophia Giovannitti in Conversation with Sarah Michelson," *Critical Correspondence*, October 12, 2021, movementresearch.org.

17 **What is art? Prostitution:** Charles Baudelaire, *Intimate Journals*, trans. Christopher Isherwood (Dover Publications, 2006), 31.

18 **Of course it was a pure fiction:** Julia Bryan-Wilson, "Dirty Commerce: Art Work and Sex Work since the 1970s," *differences* 23, no. 2 (2012): 73.

18 **The woman was paid somewhat less than her usual fee:** Ibid., 71.

18 **It was rumored:** Ibid., 73.

19 **It happens pretty often that artists, or writers, or documentary filmmakers, will want to make pornography their subject:** Johanna Fateman, Lorelei Lee, and Tiana Reid, "Virtual Roundtable," *Sublevel*, 2020, sublevelmagazine.com.

21 **Desire describes a state of attachment to something or someone:** Lauren Berlant, *Desire/Love* (punctum books, 2012), 6.

21 **I believe the difference between "escort" and "prostitute" is that:** Charlotte Shane, "Calling My Work What It Is," *Pacific Standard*, September 12, 2015, psmag.com.

22 **It appears that all of the concreteness of the world:** Tiqqun, *Preliminary Materials*, 91.

23 **There's a little rip in my brain:** Michael Clune, *White Out: The Secret Life of Heroin* (Hazelden, 2013), 6.

24 **The lenses are tiny and basically rubbish:** Hito Steyerl, *Duty Free Art* (Verso, 2017), 31.

25 **She's marrying a baby?:** *The Sopranos*, season 3, episode 12, "Amour Fou," directed by Timothy Van Patten, aired May 13, 2001, on HBO.

29 **Imagine, for example, someone who fucks like a whore:** Maggie Nelson, *Bluets* (Wave Books, 2009), 18–19.

41 **Women and girls of color, including the trafficking victims whom the criminalization of sex work:** moses moon aka thotscholar, "Symposium Introduction: Sex Workers' Rights, Advocacy, and Organizing," *Columbia Human Rights Law Review* 52, no. 3 (April 2021): 1067.

41 **listed as "arrested" for violating, NYPL § 230.00**: Queens County District Attorney's Office, "Redacted and Abridged Yang Song Investigatory Report," contributed by Melissa Gira Grant, June 21, 2018, 16, https://www.documentcloud.org/documents/4551646-Redacted-amp-Abridged-Yang-Song-Investigatory.

42 **evidence of [her] criminality**: Ibid., 22.

43 **The public is fed the racist myth**: Red Canary Song, "The Massage Parlor Means Survival Here: Red Canary Song on Robert Kraft," *Tits and Sass*, April 11, 2019, titsandsass.com.

43 **There is no human trafficking:** May Jeong, "'You Won't Believe What Happened': The Wild, Disturbing Saga of Robert Kraft's Visit to a Strip Mall Sex Spa," *Vanity Fair*, October 4, 2019, vanityfair.com.

44 **sex addiction:** Eliott C. McLaughlin, Casey Tolan and Amanda Watts, "What We Know about Robert Aaron Long, the Suspect in Atlanta Spa Shootings," *CNN*, March 18, 2021, cnn.com.

44 **The occupation [of spa work] is as common in immigrant communities as it is misunderstood:** May Jeong, "How the Atlanta Spa Shootings—the Victims, the Survivors—Tell a Story of America," *Vanity Fair*, March 14, 2022, vanityfair.com.

45 **hop[ing] to know the truth:** Melissa Gira Grant and Emma Whitford, "Family, Former Attorney of Queens Woman Who Fell to Her Death in Vice Sting Say She Was Sexually Assaulted, Pressured to Become an Informant," *The Appeal*, December 15, 2017, theappeal.org.

45 **So that's what was the most painful for me:** Zoë Lescaze, "Have We Finally Caught Up with Andrea Fraser?," *T: New York Times Style Magazine*, December 3, 2019, nytimes.com.

45 **"My first thought was, If I'm going to have to sell it, I might as well sell it," [she] said last week:** Guy Trebay, "The Way We Live Now: 6-13-04: Encounter; Sex, Art and Videotape," *New York Times Magazine*, June 13, 2004, 20.

46 **"Untitled" is about the art world:** Praxis, "Andrea Fraser," *Brooklyn Rail*, October 2004, brooklynrail.org.

46 **Andrea Fraser is a whore:** Jerry Saltz, "Critiqueus Interruptus," *Artnet*, 2007, artnet.com.

47 **never been a big fan of Fraser or her brand of institutional critique art:** Jerry Saltz, "Super Theory Woman," *Artnet*, 2004, artnet.com.

47 **Article 230 of the New York State penal code refers, quite straightforwardly:** Trebay, "Videotape."

49 **object of desire:** Berlant, *Cruel Optimism*, 23.

49 **I go on and on:** Leonard Cohen, "Other Writers," in *Book of Longing* (Ecco, 2006), 15.

50 **Every Young-Girl is an automatic, standard converter:** Tiqqun, *Preliminary Materials*, 95.

51 **I've always wanted attention:** Praxis, "Fraser."

On Violation

53 **She told me that she saw this as a business:** Angela Serino, "Role Exchange (Then and Now)," September 4, 2014, angelaserino.com.

56 **It was the cleanest drug I'd ever met:** Nan Goldin, "The Uses of Power," *Artforum*, January 2018.

56 **prostitutes drank Long Island iced tea:** Rebecca Bengal, "A Conversation with Nan Goldin on the 30th Anniversary of *The Ballad of Sexual Dependency*," *Vogue*, October 26, 2015, vogue.com.

57 **never thought of a dick in my mouth:** Rachel Rabbit White, "Cabaret," *Porn Carnival* (Wonder Press, 2019), 111.

58 **I want this chapter of my life to be over:** Charlotte Shane, "Men Consume, Women Are Consumed: 15 Thoughts on the Stigma of Sex Work," *Jezebel*, September 1, 2015, jezebel.com.

58 **There are 72 objects:** Marina Abramović, *Walk Through Walls: A Memoir* (Crown, 2016), 68.

59 **I felt really violated:** Maria Bucur, *The Century of Women: How Women Have Transformed the World since 1900* (Rowman & Littlefield, 2018), 171.

59 **A psychoanalytic model that locates the truth of a person in sexuality:** Lauren Berlant, *Desire/Love* (punctum books, 2012), 15.

60 **Before I was a sex worker, I was a fresh feminist:** Shane, "Consume."

64 **I know it's one type of power:** Charlotte Shane, Instagram post, April 2018, since deleted.

66 **How should we talk about consent:** Heather Berg, *Porn Work: Sex, Labor, and Late Capitalism* (University of North Carolina Press, 2021), 26–7.

67 **As discrimination and exploitation becomes buried:** Cancel Galleries, "How We Can Hold Art Galleries Accountable," *Hyperallergic*, January 15, 2021, hyperallergic.com.

69 **took companywide steps to address any workplace transgressions:** "*Artforum* Responds to Misconduct Complaint," *Artforum*, October 24, 2017, artforum.com.

69 **workers of the art world:** "We'll Stay Silent No More over Sexual Harassment in the Art World," *Guardian*, October 29, 2017, theguardian.com.

69 **I remember . . . two years ago . . . telling Knight:** New York County Clerk, "NYSCEF Doc. No. 158," January 22, 2021, iapps.courts.state.ny.us.

70 **to take in experiences, all of them:** *Girls*, season 2, episode 5, "One Man's Trash," directed by Richard Shepard, aired February 10, 2013, on HBO.

75 **cross-border illegal activity:** "Exclusive: Feds Raid Youngsville Business for Possible Sex, Cyber Crimes," ABC11, November 8, 2017, abc11.com.

76 **useful delinquency**: Michel Foucault, *Discipline and Punish* (Vintage Books, 1995), 280.

77 **Sex workers and survivors of trafficking, as well as advocates:** Melissa Gira Grant, "FOSTA Backers to Sex Workers: Your Work Can Never Be Safe," *The Appeal*, April 24, 2018, theappeal.org.

78 **Over the past few years, Eros has required:** Caty Simon, "The Eros Raid Means None of Us Are Safe," *Tits and Sass*, November 10, 2017, titsandsass.com.

79 **The first law limiting immigration:** Lorelei Lee, "Cash/Consent," *n+1* no. 35 (Fall 2019).

79 **convey our concerns to the Board:** Hrag Vartanian, Zachary Small, and Jasmine Weber, "Whitney Museum Staffers Demand Answers after Vice Chair's Relationship to Tear Gas Manufacturer Is Revealed," *Hyperallergic*, November 30, 2018, hyperallergic.com.

80 **While my company and the museum have distinct missions:** Alex Greenberger, "'I Am Not the Problem': Whitney Vice Chair Responds to Open Letter Calling for Action Against Him," *ARTnews*, December 3, 2018, artnews.com.

80 **made refusal seem inappropriate or impossible:** Hannah Black, Ciarán Finlayson, and Tobi Haslett, "The Tear Gas Biennial," *Artforum*, July 17, 2019, artforum.com.

81 **What does Safariland gain through its sponsorship of and association with culture:** Forensic Architecture as told to Zach Hatfield, "Forensic Architecture on Their Whitney Biennial Commission and Safariland," *Artforum*, May 13, 2019, artforum.com.

82 **Here's a man who has given a tremendous amount:** Elizabeth A. Harris and Robin Pogrebin, "Warren Kanders Quits Whitney Board after Tear Gas Protests," *New York Times*, July 25, 2019, nytimes.com.

84 **PinchukArtCentre announced that in lieu of its usual ritzy Future Generation Art Prize showcase:** Kate Sutton, "Sweet Dreaming," *Artforum*, April 22, 2022, artforum.com.

84 **toxic philanthropy of the billionaire Sackler family:** PAIN, "Home," sacklerpain.org.

85 **sex workers of all genders and demographics:** Tryst, "About," tryst.link.

93 **I have heard the argument that true intimacy cannot exist:** Jean Garnett, "Scenes from an Open Marriage," *Paris Review*, June 29, 2022, theparisreview.org.

On Legibility

95 **By presenting herself as both holy icon and object of desire:** Qualeasha Wood, *The [Black] Madonna/Whore Complex*, 2021, metmuseum.org.

95 **By centering myself in work:** Alexis Schwartz, "Qualeasha Wood Weaves Cyberculture into Tapestries," *W Magazine*, February 8, 2022, wmagazine.com.

98 **I can't wait to get into a position to make really bad art and get away with it:** Julian Spalding, "Why It's OK Not to Like Modern Art," *Times*, May 8, 2003, thetimes.co.uk.

99 **the personal-essay boom:** Jia Tolentino, "The Personal-Essay Boom Is Over," *New Yorker*, May 18, 2017, newyorker.com.

101 **an international mix of Black writers, critics, curators, and artists:** Antwaun Sargent, "Letter from Guest Editor Antwaun Sargent," *Art in America*, May 3, 2021, artnews.com.

101 **Unfortunately, as a person of color, trauma is what sells:** Schwartz, "Wood."

102 **Despite the expectation that sex workers:** Juno Mac and Molly Smith, *Revolting Prostitutes: The Fight for Sex Workers' Rights* (Verso, 2018), 3.

102 **This is not a peep show:** Melissa Gira Grant, *Playing the Whore: The Work of Sex Work* (Verso, 2014), 34.

102 **Women and authors of color or other marginalized people are often asked:** Fiona Alison Duncan, "Rachel Rabbit White Wants You to Write Poetry on the Clock," *Garage*, November 17, 2019, garage.vice.com.

103 **You cannot speak about capitalism as a person of color:** Michael Kinnucan, "An Interview with Yasmin Nair, Part Two: The Ideal Neoliberal Subject Is the Subject of Trauma," *Hypocrite Reader* 43 (August 2014).

104 **Am I a real artist?:** moses moon aka thotscholar, "A Question of Authenticity," September 7, 2020, patreon.com.

105 **I'm trying to wrap my mind around how fucked up:** moses moon aka thotscholar, November 6, 2019, twitter.com.

106 **Criminally prosecuting prostitution does not make us safer:** Jonah E. Bromwich, "Manhattan to Stop Prosecuting Prostitution, Part of Nationwide Shift," *New York Times*, April 21, 2021, nytimes.com.

108 **The spectacle is the stage at which:** Guy Debord, *The Society of the Spectacle*, trans. Ken Knabb (Bureau of Public Secrets, 2014), 16.

108 **The appalling thing isn't that the Young-Girl is fundamentally a whore:** Tiqqun, *Preliminary Materials for a Theory of the Young-Girl*, trans. Ariana Reines (Semiotext(e), 2012), 86.

109 **applied to a much older set of practices:** Gira Grant, *Playing the Whore*, 15.

109 **As traditional beliefs broke down across the 18th and 19th centuries:** William Deresiewicz, "We Need to Treat Artists as Workers, Not Decorations," *Literary Hub*, August 5, 2020, lithub.com.

109 **The corralling of these incongruent identities:** Julia Bryan-Wilson, "Dirty Commerce: Art Work and Sex Work since the 1970s," *differences* 23, no. 2 (2012): 84.

110 **During the presentations of *Site*, my own kinetic theater:** Carolee Schneemann, "Robert Morris," *Artforum*, February 2019.

111 **If you want to paint, put your clothes back on:** Steve Rose, "Carolee Schneemann: 'I Never Thought I Was Shocking,'" *Guardian*, March 10, 2014, theguardian.com.

111 **male critics:** Holland Cotter, "Shock of the Nude," *New York Times*, February 1, 2018, nytimes.com.

111 **I needed to see if I could re-proportion:** Robert Enright, "Notes on Fuseology," *Border Crossings*, December 2014.

112 **display of female flesh:** Bryan-Wilson, "Dirty Commerce," 87.

112 **the control afforded through the act of self-imaging:** Aria Dean, "Closing the Loop," *New Inquiry*, March 1, 2016, thenewinquiry.com.

113 **the most famous example . . . of what Judith Wilson calls:** Lorraine O'Grady, "Olympia's Maid: Reclaiming Black Female Subjectivity," 1992, 1994, lorraineogrady.com.

114 **[the work is] not . . . pornographic . . . because an art work:** Kirsten Strom, "'Made in Heaven': Politics, Art and Pornography," *Iowa Journal of Cultural Studies* 17, no. 1 (1998): 55.

114 **advertising for a porno film:** Anthony Haden-Guest, "Art or Commerce?," *Vanity Fair*, November 1, 1991, vanityfair.com.

115 **To have a family based on Protestant values:** Warren St. John, "Scenes from a Marriage," *New Yorker*, December 11, 1994, newyorker.com.

115 **trying to share . . . transcendence with the viewer:** "Jeff Koons Destroying 'Made in Heaven,'" Reserve Channel, youtube.com.

115 **that art is incomplete without the perceptual and emotional involvement of the viewer:** Eric R. Kandel, "What the Brain Can Tell Us about Art," *New York Times*, April 12, 2013, nytimes.com.

117 **I'm told (often with a note of dismissive acceptance) that parading a nude female:** Nick Messitte, "G I R L meets N.E.R.D.—The Second Adolescence of Pharrell," *Forbes*, February 28, 2014, forbes.com.

118 **that these images are not pornographic:** Strom, "'Heaven,'" 56.

118 **carefully detail/describe one Black gURL's #identity + xxxperience of sex and pop culture online:** Kimberly Drew, "Towards a New Digital Landscape," *Sightlines*, May 11, 2015, walkerart.org.

118 **Holloway edited videos and photographs:** Tiana Reid, "The Promiscuity of Power: Shawné Michaelain Holloway," *Art in America*, August 6, 2020, artnews.com.

119 **I hosted it there partially because I don't feel that it's right to just scoop:** Allan Gardner, "'Can't Stay in Your BDSM Hole Forever': Shawné Michaelain Holloway," *Quietus*, September 1, 2018, thequietus.com.

119 **This job is not forgettable:** Lorelei Lee, "Once You Have Made Pornography," May 11, 2017, medium.com.

121 **As the industry's slang term:** Linda Williams, *Hard Core: Power, Pleasure, and the "Frenzy of the Visible"* (University of California Press, 1989), 106.

123 **Am I a narcissist?:** Steve Kettman, "The Narcissist," *LA Weekly*, October 11, 2000, laweekly.com.

123 **Merritt's blow job pictures:** David Bowman, "'Digital Diaries,'" *Salon*, May 6, 2000, salon.com.

123 **I can't separate them:** Natacha Merritt, *Digital Diaries* (Taschen: 2000), 216.

124 **an almost religious aura:** David Everitt Howe, "Paul Mpagi Sepuya," *Art in America*, May 1, 2019, artnews.com.

124 **To make visible a lot of these latent indexical traces:** Art Basel, *Meet the Artists: Paul Mpagi Sepuya*, October 7, 2019, youtube.com.

125 **I spotted one of your photographs on Scruff:** Giancarlo Montes Santangelo, "Q&A: Paul Mpagi Sepuya," *Strange Fire*, November 21, 2019, strangefirecollective.com.

126 **overtly sexual or pornographic material:** Kari Paul, "No, Apple's New Policy Doesn't Mean It's Banning Grindr," *Guardian*, June 15, 2021, theguardian.com.

126 **advertising massage or escort services:** SCRUFF Team, "Profile Guidelines," Scruff Support, support.scruff.com.

126 **looking for loads:** Rob Salerno, "US Customs Block Canadian Man after Reading His Scruff Profile," *Xtra*, February 20, 2017, xtramagazine.com.

127 **But it is the girl's expression:** Bowman, "Digital."

127 **Sepuya photographs himself:** Howe, "Sepuya."

128 **Seedbed might have made my career, but it also destroyed it:** Jeff Rian, "Vito Acconci," *Purple* 21 (2014), purple.fr.

128 **Half-way across the room:** Germano Celant, "'Dirty Acconci,'" *Artforum*, November 1980, artforum.com.

128 **Did you really ever have an orgasm under the Seedbed?:** Richard Prince, "Vito Acconci by Richard Prince," *Bomb Magazine*, July 1, 1991, bombmagazine.org.

128 **Could you find it sexy?:** Shelley Jackson, "A Conversation with Vito Acconci," *Culture*, January 1, 2007, culture.org.

128 **All art is pornography:** Celant, "'Dirty.'"

129 **How intimate or self-revelatory can art be, and still be art and not life?:** April Kingsley, "Reviews and Previews," *ARTNews*, March 1972.

129 **A conversation in which a man keeps touching a woman's arm:** Prince, "Acconci."

131 **I am almost not an "I" anymore:** Vito Acconci, *Following Piece*, 1969, metmuseum.org.

131 **It really was an amazing photograph:** Roberta Smith, "Art or Ad or What? It Caused a Lot of Fuss," *New York Times*, July 24, 2009, nytimes.com.

132 **According to Benglis, *Artforum* insisted:** Richard Meyer, "Bone of Contention," *Artforum*, November 2004.

132 **For the first time in the 13 years:** Lawrence Alloway, Max Kozloff, Rosalind Krauss, Joseph Masheck, and Annette Michelson, "Letters," *Artforum*, December 1974.

133 **the art-star system, and the way artists use themselves:** Meyer, "Bone."

133 **Critics and curators tend:** Ibid.

133 **pornography is the theory, and rape the practice:** Robin Morgan, *Going Too Far: The Personal Chronicle of a Feminist* (Vintage Books, 1978), 169.

133 **really studying pornography:** Meyer, "Bone."

133 **I don't want to be part of a movement that has a sense of priorities:** Hallie Lieberman, "If You Mold It, They Will Come," *Bitch Media*, February 13, 2019, bitchmedia.org.

133 **men use the penis to deliver death to women:** Andrea Dworkin, *Intercourse: The Twentieth Anniversary Edition* (Basic Books, 2007), 239.

134 **She's performing gender, not performing "male":** Katy Diamond Hamer, "26 Female Artists on Lynda Benglis and the Art World's Gender Problems (NSFW)," *Vulture*, November 23, 2014, vulture.com.

134 **social and economic exclusivity and inequality:** Ibid.

135 **drawing on Victorian-era pornography and turning it inside out:** Tiana Reid, "Tourmaline," *4Columns*, January 22, 2021, 4columns.org.

135 **Black-owned pleasure gardens:** Cyrus Simonoff, "Earthly Delights," *Artforum*, January 14, 2021, artforum.com.

135 **walking while trans:** Emma Whitford, "When Walking While Trans Is a Crime," *The Cut*, thecut.com.

135 **loitering with intent to commit prostitution:** Mary Harris, "Sex Workers Want More Than Just the Right to Work," *Slate*, May 4, 2021, slate.com.

136 **People always think of a trans woman**: Whitford, "Walking."

136 **[During] my formative years in New York:** Coco Romack, "Honey Dijon, Juliana Huxtable, and Nomi Ruiz Affirm the Sacred, Shamanistic Pleasures of Sex and Sound," *Document Journal*, December 10, 2010, documentjournal.com.

136 **Sex workers and anyone perceived to be a sex worker:** Gira Grant, *Playing the Whore*, 9.

136 **Part of this exhibition has been the experience of me going to Chapter Gallery's pop-up:** Simonoff, "Delights."

137 **I think artists create their own rules:** Anna McNay, "Lynda Benglis: 'I Think Artists Create Their Own Rules,'" *Studio International*, February 16, 2015, studiointernational.com.

138 **I can't wait till I'm invited to talk about white supremacy-related stuff and people stop calling me an "activist":** Zoé Samudzi, August 2020, twitter.com, since deleted.

138 **People do this to me all the time:** Aruna D'Souza, August 2020, twitter.com, since deleted.

139 **We permit some violence against women to be committed:** Gira Grant, *Playing the Whore*, 6.

140 **I put some humour into the women's movement:** Skye Sherwin, "Glitter, Latex and Double Dildos: Art Provocateur Lynda Benglis Relives Her Rollercoaster Career," *Guardian*, October 6, 2017, theguardian.com.

On Meaning, Part II

141 **Because you are close:** Leonard Cohen, "Owning Everything," in *The Spice-Box of Earth* (McClelland & Stewart, 2018), 34.

141 **Desire and knowledge (body and mind):** Samuel Delany, *Times Square Red, Times Square Blue* (New York University Press, 1999), 168–9.

141 **What does love mean:** Adrienne Rich, "Phantasia for Elvira Shatayev," *The Dream of a Common Language: Poems 1974–1977* (W. W. Norton & Company, 1993), 6.

142 **The strong women told the faggots that there are two important things:** Larry Mitchell, *The Faggots and Their Friends between Revolutions* (Calamus Books, 1977), 21.

142 **When refusing their imposed disposability:** M. E. O'Brien, "Junkie Communism," *Commune*, July 15, 2019, communemag.com.

142 **The potflower on the windowsill:** Muriel Rukeyser, "The Power of Suicide," in *The Speed of Darkness* (Vintage Books, 1971), 38.

143 **an expanded collective of sex workers against work:** Clandestine Whores Network, "Beneath Everything," *Pinko*, October 15, 2019, pinko.online.

146 **what do we actually *mean* when we say "sex work is work"?:** moses moon aka thotscholar, *Heauxthots: On Terminology, and Other [Un]important Things* (bbydoll press, 2019), 19.

147 **If we all spit together we can drown the bastards:** Gregor Gall, "Loved by the Workers, Feared by the Bosses," *Jacobin*, May 1, 2017, jacobin.com.

148 **[existence] is now nothing but a *lifelong* struggle:** Tiqqun, *Preliminary Materials for a Theory of the Young-Girl*, trans. Ariana Reines (Semiotext(e), 2012), 13–14.

148 **I am a man, I'm here:** *The Wire*, season 4, episode 4, "Refugees," directed by Jim McKay, aired October 1, 2006, on HBO.

149 **Relations of power are not in a position of exteriority with respect to other types of relationships:** Michel Foucault, *The History of Sexuality, Volume I: An Introduction* (Pantheon Books, 1978), 94.

152 **work-life harmony:** Katie Canales and Zoë Bernard, "Why Jeff Bezos Doesn't Believe in Work-Life Balance: 'It Actually Is a Circle,'" *Insider*, November 22, 2021, businessinsider.com.

152 **I would rather go back to a state correctional facility:** Michael Sainato, "'I'm Not a Robot': Amazon Workers Condemn Unsafe, Grueling Conditions at Warehouse," *Guardian*, February 5, 2020, theguardian.com.

152 **I want to consider *life* as a possible counterpoint to work:** Kathi Weeks, *The Problem with Work: Feminism, Marxism, Antiwork Politics, and Postwork Imaginaries* (Duke University Press, 2011), 230.

152 **recuperated into the logic of commodity culture:** Ibid., 231.

152 **to be continually invented:** Ibid., 232.

153 **get a life:** Ibid., 231.

153 **though it is a life that would be ours:** Ibid., 233.

154 **queerness is not quite here:** José Esteban Muñoz, *Cruising Utopia: The Then and There of Queer Futurity* (New York University Press, 2009), 21.

154 **dream and enact new and better pleasures:** Ibid., 1.

154 **is even more fun than going to San Sebastian:** Ibid., 5–7.

157 **I sit down at the table:** David Leon Chandler, *Brothers in Blood: The Rise of the Criminal Brotherhoods* (Dutton, 1975), 19.

160 **if what you want is jobs:** Diane di Prima, *Revolutionary Letters* (City Lights Books, 2021), 28.